Collins

11+
Stretch &
Challenge

Activities & Tests

Phil Marchant, Shelley Welsh
and Beatrix Woodhead

Acknowledgements

Published by Collins
An imprint of HarperCollins*Publishers*
1 London Bridge Street
London SE1 9GF

HarperCollins*Publishers*
1st Floor, Watermarque Building,
Ringsend Road, Dublin 4, Ireland

ISBN: 978-0-00-848393-7

First published 2022

10 9 8 7 6 5 4 3 2 1

Publishers: Sundus Pasha and Clare Souza
Authors: Phil Marchant, Shelley Welsh and Beatrix Woodhead
With thanks to Chris Pearse at Teachitright for additional authoring and support
Project Management: Richard Toms
Cover Design: Sarah Duxbury
Inside Concept Design: Ian Wrigley
Typesetting and artwork: Jouve India Private Limited
Production: Karen Nulty
Printed in the United Kingdom by Martins the Printers

MIX
Paper from
responsible sources
FSC™ C007454

www.fsc.org

This book is produced from independently certified FSC™ paper to ensure responsible forest management.

For more information visit:
www.harpercollins.co.uk/green

Contents

What are the CEM 11+ tests?

CEM 11+ tests are developed by the Centre for Evaluation and Monitoring, which is part of Cambridge Assessment and Cambridge University Press. They were introduced following concerns that 11+ tests had become too easy to coach and this approach would avoid 'teaching to the test'. In addition, it would reduce the predictability of content in the assessments. CEM tests have now become popular across many regions of the UK.

What do the CEM tests involve?

CEM tests are broadly aligned with Key Stage 2 National Curriculum content. CEM papers are mixed, covering verbal, non-verbal and numerical ability. The verbal ability sections focus on word-related questions, comprehension and cloze skills. The table below gives more detail on the topics covered.

Subject area	Content
Verbal Ability: English comprehension	An extract (either fiction, non-fiction or poetry) followed by a series of questions.
Verbal Ability: Cloze passages	Passages with omitted words/letters and presented in different styles: word bank, multiple-choice word options or partial words.
Verbal Ability: Word choice	A series of word-related question types. These might include synonyms, antonyms, homonyms, shuffled sentences or definition questions.
Numerical Ability	Questions covering a range of mathematical topics, testing both numeracy and problem-solving skills.
Non-Verbal Reasoning (NVR) and Spatial Reasoning	Typically, NVR questions include matrices, series, odd one out, analogies and finding the figure that is most alike. Spatial reasoning question types could involve cubes and nets, composite shapes, 2D views of 3D shapes and 3D rotation.

How are the CEM papers structured?

Candidates usually take two papers (approximately 45 minutes in length) that are split into several short sections. These sections move from one subject to another, for example, from mathematical problem solving to word choice. Timings are allocated to each section and, once the time elapses, children cannot return to that section again. The timings are challenging (for example, 15 minutes for a comprehension test of 20 questions or 7 minutes for a word-choice test of 16 questions).

Furthermore, questions can be open or multiple-choice, with answers being written on a separate sheet. Often there are more questions given than the time will allow to be answered. CEM 11+ tests are often CD administered and the audio guides the candidates through the different sections. See page 7 for more information about the answer sheets.

How can you support your child's preparations?

The CEM tests require excellent vocabulary skills and therefore it is important that your child develops a rich word knowledge. It is recommended that children keep a record of unfamiliar words that they find in their reading materials or practice resources. Writing a short definition and placing it in a sentence will also help them to use the word in context. Here are some more suggestions for word-building activities:

- **Playing word games** can really enhance vocabulary. Children learn words while having fun at the same time. Examples include bananagrams, *Scrabble*™, *Boggle*™, crosswords and word wheels.
- **Reading widely** with your child and using 'powerful' words in everyday conversation.
- **Turning on subtitles** on the television can help children to pick up new words.
- **Collecting words** from a range of different word classes can support retention, e.g. homophones, compound words or homonyms.
- **Challenge your child** to find synonyms and antonyms for specific words. For example, how many words can you find that mean the same as '*quick*'?
- **Flashcards** can be used to expose children to more challenging vocabulary, which will give them an advantage in the 11+ test. Repeating the process of showing the words can help with retention.
- **Imagery** is an excellent way to support word-building. Having an image of a word can really support children who prefer visual stimulus to learn new vocabulary.

English comprehension is a prominent part of the CEM tests. Children should read a wide variety of genres and be prepared to read both classic literature and contemporary pieces. The comprehension exercise can include questions on inference and deduction, fact and opinion, and vocabulary. Learning the meaning of key literacy devices such as personification, simile, metaphor, onomatopoeia and alliteration will help your child to identify them within the passage. Another useful preparation strategy is to become familiar with all the different word groups, including prepositions, abstract nouns and adverbs.

Numerical reasoning skills are another integral part of the CEM tests. Children need a solid foundation of basic arithmetic and should be able to use efficient methods for all four operations. The questions are often presented in a word-problem format, with concepts that might include:

- Percentages, decimals and fractions
- Measurement
- Averages
- Ratio and proportion
- Data handling (tables, pictograms, pie charts, bar or line graphs, Venn or Carroll diagrams)
- Algebra
- Coordinates
- Angles
- 2D and 3D shapes
- Area and perimeter
- Knowledge of number
- Rotational symmetry
- Volume

Children need to learn key mathematical terminology to support their numerical ability. An 11+ maths glossary can help them to revise key terms.

Non-verbal and **spatial reasoning** are rarely covered at primary school and therefore gaining familiarity with the different style of questions is strongly recommended. Good visualisaton skills are crucial, including being able to spot similarities and differences between figures. Supporting tasks, such as those listed below, can enhance non-verbal reasoning and spatial understanding:

- Completing 'spot the difference' puzzles can sharpen the type of skills required in non-verbal reasoning exercises.
- Playing games such as *Tetris* can support children with rotation, which is a key variable in this subject.
- Asking a friend or family member to draw a picture. The child then tries to copy the image, so it is an exact reflection.
- Making sure children know the difference between clockwise and anti-clockwise.
- Creating a net to form a cube that can be drawn on, to show the relationship between the faces, is an excellent resource to help with cube and net questions.
- Learning key vocabulary associated with non-verbal reasoning (e.g. different types of shading such as hatching, bold fill, spotted) helps children to understand what they are looking for.

Developing good exam technique is imperative in CEM 11+ tests as your child will be under challenging time conditions. Spending too long on one question will cost precious seconds, so children should move on to the next one to make sure they answer enough questions. Success is dependent upon having plenty of timed practice to help to replicate test conditions and therefore making your child feel more comfortable on the day.

On the days before the test and the actual 11+ test day

The final few days before the actual test are a crucial time. By this stage of the preparation, your child should feel they have covered all the areas. Thus, it is more about managing expectations and the emotions involved. Reviewing any specific 11+ subjects or topics is fine, but cramming and last-minute preparation may cause panic. Help your child (and you!) to relax by planning a fun activity to take their mind off the test and reduce any nerves.

Here are some other practical tips:
- Always be calm yourself – any sign of anxiety in you or your manner will transfer itself to your child. If you are calm, happy and relaxed, then they will stand a chance of being the same.
- The night before, collect everything required for the test. This should include a bottle of water, any stationery allowed and particularly things like glasses or medication. This should prevent a mad rush on the morning of the test.
- Encourage your child to wear comfortable clothes as they do not want to be distracted by feeling uncomfortable during the test. Wearing several layers of clothing will allow them to adjust their temperature as necessary.
- Make sure your child has a good breakfast and drinks properly. Try to avoid overly sugary breakfast cereals. Sometimes parents want to give their child a treat on the morning of the test and so give them their favourite sugary breakfast, but this is likely to set them on edge due to excess energy levels.
- It is a very good idea to arrive at the test venue early so your child doesn't feel worried about being late. Having a little walk can make all the difference.
- Mornings can be rushed and any tension will be communicated to your child. Any urgency to get up, get dressed, wash, get to the car, annoyance with other drivers, etc. all adds unduly to the pressure. Try to avoid it.

- A few reminders can help your child to keep focused on the task in hand. These might include: remember to use your time wisely; use any strategies learnt; apply a process of elimination on multiple-choice answer options where necessary; and never leave any answers blank.
- Before they enter the hall or classroom, advise your child not to talk too much to others about the tests. If others are nervous, this could rub off on your own child.
- It is not unusual for children to be sick, to cry, to keep lifting their hand or to want to go to the toilet during the test. In many sections of the test, children will need to answer one question about every 30 seconds, so even the slightest distraction can have an effect. If children are prepared to expect distractions, then they may well be less affected by events.

Using the multiple-choice sheet

It is crucial to use the multiple-choice sheet correctly and be systematic with recording answers. Below are some important points to remember:

- The multiple-choice papers have answer booklets that look like a lottery sheet. There tends to be at least four possible answers for each question and your child will be required to draw a single horizontal pencil line next to their choice.
- Concentrate on neatness throughout the exam, as an unclear answer will result in a lost mark.
- Always record one answer at a time.
- Circle unanswered questions clearly so they are easily visible and go back at the end to attempt them if there is time.
- Only mark the answer on the multiple-choice sheet.
- Ensure all markings are clear as these sheets are often marked by an optical reader.
- Check the answer correlates to the question (it can be easy to mark the incorrect answer).
- If a mistake is made, it needs to be rubbed out and **not** crossed out. It will be read as 'wrong' if there are two marks where there should only be one.
- Do not spend too much time fretting over a particularly difficult question as this will cost valuable minutes. Move on and go back later if there is time.
- Check all answers at the end of the section if there is time. Go back to unanswered questions.
- Attempt all questions. Should your child still not know an answer even when they revisit the question, they should have a go as there is a chance it could be correct.

How to Use this Book

This book will take your child's preparations for the 11+ CEM test to the next level with activities and test papers that are designed to stretch and challenge them. Working at an advanced level during preparation will help your child to increase their attainment, build their confidence and give them an edge on the big day.

In the first part of the book, your child can work through colourful, spread-based activities for the topics that candidates often find the hardest to grasp. The topics are organised into these three core areas of the CEM tests – Numerical Ability, Verbal Ability and Non-Verbal Ability – and consist of a series of engaging activities with added difficulty to challenge your child's ability and stretch their skills.

Before moving on, your child can recap and refine their skills by taking on a bank of mixed activities at the end of each of the Numerical Ability, Verbal Ability and Non-Verbal Ability sections.

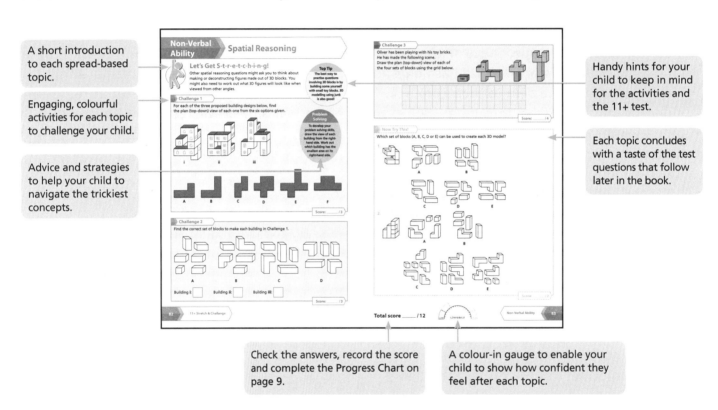

A short introduction to each spread-based topic.

Engaging, colourful activities for each topic to challenge your child.

Advice and strategies to help your child to navigate the trickiest concepts.

Handy hints for your child to keep in mind for the activities and the 11+ test.

Each topic concludes with a taste of the test questions that follow later in the book.

Check the answers, record the score and complete the Progress Chart on page 9.

A colour-in gauge to enable your child to show how confident they feel after each topic.

In the second part of the book, three test papers enable your child to tackle challenging questions under timed conditions. To mirror the experience of the 11+ test, answer sheets are provided at the very back of the book. Further copies of these answer sheets can be downloaded from **collins.co.uk/11plus** to enable them to be used again and again.

Answers for all questions are at the back of the book. Your child will need separate sheets of paper to answer some of the questions.

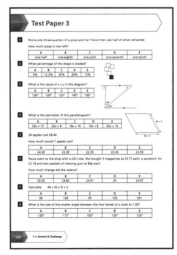

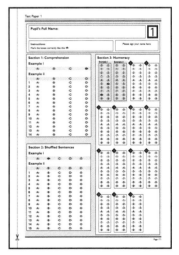

Record your scores on these charts. Convert each score to a percentage (divide your score by the total and multiply by 100). Then colour in the percentage score in each bar of the chart to compare your results and show your success.

Progress Charts

Numerical Ability Activities	Your score	%	10	20	30	40	50	60	70	80	90	100
Number and Place Value	/26											
Operations	/32											
Fractions, Decimals and Percentages	/27											
Ratio and Proportion	/17											
Perimeter and Area	/16											
Geometry	/13											
Algebra	/22											
Simultaneous Equations	/22											
Mean, Median, Mode and Range	/20											
Statistics	/16											
Mixed Activities	/25											

Verbal Ability Activities	Your score	%	10	20	30	40	50	60	70	80	90	100
How Does an Author Create Atmosphere?	/26											
Characterisation	/37											
Inference, Deduction and Rhetorical Devices	/26											
Spelling	/38											
Grammar	/29											
Word Definitions	/22											
Odd One Out	/21											
Synonyms and Antonyms	/20											
Word Association	/21											
Cloze	/25											
Shuffled Sentences	/26											
Mixed Activities	/55											

Non-Verbal Ability Activities	Your score	%	10	20	30	40	50	60	70	80	90	100
Making Connections	/13											
Finding Relationships	/14											
Spotting Patterns	/12											
Completing Sequences	/12											
Breaking Codes 1	/8											
Breaking Codes 2	/7											
Paper Folding	/14											
Cubes and Nets	/23											
Rotations and Reflections	/10											
Hidden and Composite Shapes	/17											
Spatial Reasoning	/12											
Mixed Activities	/19											

Test Paper 1	Your score	%	10	20	30	40	50	60	70	80	90	100
	/89											

Test Paper 2	Your score	%	10	20	30	40	50	60	70	80	90	100
	/88											

Test Paper 3	Your score	%	10	20	30	40	50	60	70	80	90	100
	/89											

Let's Get S-t-r-e-t-c-h-i-n-g!

The place value of each digit of a number tells you how much that digit is worth.

So in the number 213:

- 2 is the hundreds value
- 1 is the tens value
- 3 is the ones value.

Challenge 1

a) Which digit is the tens value of the number 248? ....

b) Which digit is the hundreds value of the number 381? ....

c) Which digit is the hundreds value of the number 6,498? ....

d) Which digit is the tens value of the number 51,724? ....

e) Which digit is the thousands value of the number 58,293? ....

f) Which digit is the ten thousands value of the number 225,923? ....

Score: _____ /6

Problem Solving

It's important to understand place value so that you recognise the value of digits and numbers. Take particular note of places before and after a decimal point. For example, don't mix up the hundreds place and the hundredths place.

Challenge 2

a) Which digit is in the ones place in the number 7,409.34?

....

b) Which digit is in the ten thousands place in the number 35,352.94?

....

c) Which digit is in the hundreds place in the number 19,304.55?

....

d) Which digit is in the hundredths place in the number 18,204.53? ....

e) Which digit is in the hundred thousands place in the number 2,312,353.483? ....

f) Which digit is in the thousandths place in the number 24.2914? ....

Score: _____ /6

Challenge 3

Work out:

a) 2.9 + 4.2 _____

b) 3.04 + 4.17 _____

c) 5.05 – 4.28 _____

d) 9.25 – 5.38 _____

e) 14.28 + 9.32 _____

Score: _____ / 5

Challenge 4

Work out:

a) 2.4825 × 100 _____

b) 0.395 × 1,000 _____

c) 485 × 2.5 _____

d) 3,025.24 ÷ 10 _____

e) 5,394.218 ÷ 100 _____

f) 0.414 ÷ 1,000 _____

Top Tip

When multiplying a decimal number by 10, 100 or 1,000, count the number of zeros and move the decimal point that many places to the right. When dividing a decimal number by 10, 100 or 1,000, count the number of zeros and move the decimal point that many places to the left. So, for example, 7.98 × 10 = 79.8 and 654 ÷ 100 = 6.54

Score: _____ / 6

Now Try This!

1. Kevin did a tough calculation on his calculator that resulted in the number 52,481.3952

    He then had to multiply it by 0.01. What number did this result in?

    A 52.4813952 **B** 5.24813952 **C** 524.813952 **D** 5,248.13952 **E** 52,481.3952

2. If 2.84 × 14.32 = 40.6688, work out:

    a) 28.4 × 1.432

    A 40.6688 **B** 406.688 **C** 4.06688 **D** 0.406688 **E** 4,066.88

    b) 284 × 0.1432

    A 4,066.88 **B** 4.06688 **C** 406.688 **D** 0.406688 **E** 40.6688

Score: _____ / 3

Total score _____ / 26

LOW   CONFIDENCE   HIGH

Numerical Ability

Operations

Let's Get S-t-r-e-t-c-h-i-n-g!

The four mathematical operations you will need to work with are addition (+), multiplication (×), subtraction (−) and division (÷). Addition is the inverse (opposite) of subtraction. Multiplication is the inverse of division. For example:

$$50 \times 5 = 250 \quad \text{and} \quad 250 \div 5 = 50$$

Problem Solving

Operations are the fundamentals of maths so make sure you master them as well as you can. Many problems in the 11+ tests will require you to translate the words into mathematical operations.

Challenge 1

a) Work out sixty-eight plus seventeen.

b) Calculate 249 + 64

c) What is 338 minus 39?

d) What is 8,446 − 3,978?

e) Calculate 924 + 157

f) Calculate 4,772 + 13,593

g) Calculate one hundred and thirty-three minus fifty-six.

h) Calculate 6,482 − 3,826

Score: _____ / 8

Challenge 2

a) What is twelve multiplied by nineteen?

b) What is 405 divided by 25?

c) Calculate 307 × 20.5

d) Calculate 900 ÷ 36

e) Calculate 208 × 48

f) What is four hundred and thirty-two divided by eighteen?

g) Calculate 62.4 × 29.5

h) Calculate 84.7 + 32

Score: _____ / 8

Fill in the gaps in this table:

23		7	=	161
	+	346	=	1,071
77			=	7
64	×		=	0.64
1.5	×	0.5	=	
300		0.25	=	75
	÷	5	=	80
10,000	×		=	1
0.352	×		=	352
0.5	÷		=	0.25

Problem Solving

Remember that you can use inverse operations to find a number that is missing on the left side of the equals sign.

Score: _____ / 11

a) Chloe has some marbles. She organises them in 14 rows, with 13 marbles in each row.

How many marbles does Chloe have in total? _____

b) Pete has £217. He buys an item for £25 and another for £46.

How much money does he have left? _____

c) Azeem's phone company charges him 25p a minute for the first 20 minutes of a call, then 15p for every minute thereafter. Azeem makes a 38-minute phone call.

How much does the call cost him? _____

Top Tip

Some word questions may require you to use more than one operation. Working step-by-step, use the appropriate operation for each calculation. It helps to separate out your calculations to avoid making mistakes.

Score: _____ / 3

Now Try This!

1. What is three thousand two hundred and twenty-nine minus six hundred and eighty-two?

   A 2,547   B 2,537   C 1,646   D 2,447   E 2,548

2. There were 483 people on the train. 265 of them were paying the full fare at £3.50. The remainder all had a half-price voucher that they were using.

   What was the total cost of the fares for all the people on the train?

   A £1,212   B £1,215   C £1,429   D £1,309   E £1,209

Score: _____ / 2

Total score _____ / 32

LOW   CONFIDENCE   HIGH

Numerical Ability   13

Let's Get S-t-r-e-t-c-h-i-n-g!

The same value of proportion can be expressed as a fraction, decimal or percentage. So $\frac{1}{2}$ is the fraction, 0.5 the decimal and 50% the percentage.

Challenge 1

Fill in the empty spaces in the table.

Fraction	Decimal	Percentage
	0.5	50
	0.25	
		40
$\frac{1}{5}$	0.2	
		10
	0.45	
$\frac{7}{25}$		
		22%

Top Tip

If you have the percentage and need to know the decimal, simply divide the percentage by 100. So to get the percentage from a decimal, simply multiply the decimal by 100.

Score: _____ /14

Challenge 2

a) What is $\frac{6}{50}$ as a decimal? ....

b) What is 0.4 as a fraction in its simplest form? ....

c) What is $\frac{3}{5}$ as a percentage? ....

d) What is $\frac{5}{8}$ as a percentage? ....

e) What is 0.15 as a fraction in its simplest form? ....

f) What is 60% as a fraction in its simplest form? ....

g) What is 1 as a percentage? ....

Top Tip

To get a decimal from a fraction, divide the top number by the bottom number.

Top Tip

To get a percentage from a fraction, divide the top number by the bottom number and then multiply by 100.

Score: _____ /7

Challenge 3

a) What fraction of this shape is shaded grey?

Simplify the fraction as far as possible.

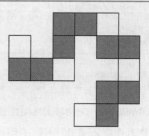

_____

b) What percentage of this shape
is shaded grey?

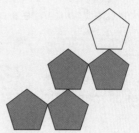

_____

Score: _____ / 2

Challenge 4

a) Shade in 40% of this shape:

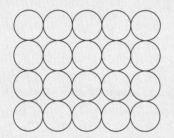

b) Shade in 0.2 of this shape:

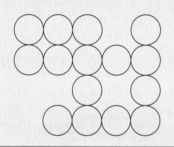

Score: _____ / 2

Problem Solving

If you are told the percentage and one half of the proportion (such as 20 of the bricks in the wall were blue, which was 80% of the whole wall) but need to work out the missing part of the proportion, substitute x into your formula.

So, to find out how many bricks are in the wall, we know that $\frac{20}{x} = \frac{80}{100}$.

Multiply both sides by 100 to get

$\frac{2,000}{x} = 80$, so $x = \frac{2,000}{80}$

$= 25$ bricks

Now Try This!

1. 6,500 people went to the beach on a sunny bank holiday. Three-fifths of them were wearing a hat. 35% of those not wearing a hat were wearing sunglasses.

   How many people at the beach were not wearing a hat but wearing sunglasses?

   A 950　　　　B 940　　　　C 945　　　　D 910　　　　E 850

2. Min achieved 55% in an exam. His friend Lou scored 65%.

   If Min got 33 marks, how many more marks did Lou get?

   A 5　　　　B 7　　　　C 4　　　　D 6　　　　E 8

Score: _____ / 2

Total score _____ / 27

LOW　CONFIDENCE　HIGH

Let's Get S-t-r-e-t-c-h-i-n-g!

A ratio shows the relationship between two or more numbers or quantities. So if I get twice as much pizza as my friend, our ratio of pizza is 2 : 1. The colon just means 'to'. Ratios can be used to divide a quantity and find the different proportions of it.

Challenge 1

a) Jim has four times as many stickers as Leroy.

What is the ratio of stickers between Jim and Leroy? ....

b) In a bag, there are 8 red marbles for every 7 blue marbles.

What is the ratio of red to blue marbles? ....

c) Sam and Chris have earned £24, which they split in the ratio 3 : 1.

How much money does Sam get? ....

d) Phil is twice as old as Kiran, who is three times as old as Lucy.

What is the ratio of their ages? ....

Score: _____ / 4

Challenge 2

a) Edith is six times older than Ritu. Their combined ages are 42.

How old is Edith? ....

b) Wayne and Clara have saved £90 between them.
They divide it in the ratio of 5 : 4.

How much money does Clara end up with?

....

c) There are 98 children in an assembly hall, with a ratio between boys and girls of 4 : 3.

How many girls are in the assembly hall?

Problem Solving

If £77 is divided between Liam and Pete in the ratio 4 : 3, you can find out how much they each get as follows. Add the parts of the ratio (4 + 3 = 7) and then divide 77 by that 7 to get 11. To get Liam's amount, multiply 11 by his part of the ratio (4) to get £44. Pete would get 11 times his part of the ratio (3) to get £33. As a check, £44 + £33 does equal the total of £77 so we have proportioned properly.

Score: _____ / 3

Challenge 3

Fill in the spaces in this table for the different classes in a year group.

Boys	Girls	Ratio
15	20	3 : 4
12	18	
8	10	
6		2 : 5
28		7 : 4

Problem Solving

Simplify the ratio where it is possible to divide both parts by their highest common factor. For example, to simplify 10 : 12, divide both numbers by their highest common factor of 2 to obtain 5 : 6.

Score: _____ / 4

Challenge 4

a) Charlie has four times as many stickers as Asif, who has three times as many stickers as Lucy.

How would you express this as a ratio? _____

Problem Solving

Don't worry if there are more than two proportions to be worked out. Using the ratio, follow the same technique as shown in the Problem Solving tip on page 16 to calculate each proportion.

b) Carole has three times as much money as James.
Mark has twice as much money as Carole.
They have £500 between them.

How much money does Carole have? _____

c) Jason has six times the amount of savings as Wayne. Lennie has twice as much as Jason.

If they have £228 saved between them, how much does Wayne have saved? _____

d) Robert has half as many games as Ranjeet. Helen has three times as many games as Ranjeet.
They have 63 games between them in total.

How many games does Ranjeet have? _____

Score: _____ / 4

Now Try This!

1. There are 200 cricket clubs in a county. A quarter of them have only one team.
   Of the remainder, twice as many clubs have exactly two teams than have more than two.
   How many of the cricket clubs in the county have exactly two teams?

   A 120   **B** 50   **C** 100   **D** 80   **E** 90

2. In Jack's drawer, there are 5 pairs of socks for every pair of pants.
   If you were to draw a pie chart of this information, what angle size would you use for pants?

   A 50 degrees   **B** 60 degrees   **C** 75 degrees   **D** 65 degrees   **E** 45 degrees

Score: _____ / 2

Total score _____ / 17

LOW   CONFIDENCE   HIGH

Perimeter and Area

Let's Get S-t-r-e-t-c-h-i-n-g!

The perimeter of a shape is the distance around it. So, the perimeter of a square with width 2 cm is: $2 + 2 + 2 + 2 = 8\,cm$

The area is the entire space enclosed within the perimeter. It is always measured in square units. So the area of the square shown here is calculated by length × width: $2 × 2 = 4\,cm^2$

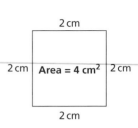

2 cm

2 cm | Area = 4 cm² | 2 cm

2 cm

Challenge 1

a) A square has a width of 10 cm.

What is the perimeter of the square? ....

b) A rectangle has a width of 6 cm and a length of 8 cm.

What is the perimeter of the rectangle? ....

c) What is the perimeter of this shape?

....

8 cm

24 cm

Score: _____ / 3

Challenge 2

a) A square has a width of 7 cm.

What is the area of the square?
Make sure you include the correct units. ....

b) A rectangle has a width of 9 cm and a length of 12 cm.

What is the area of the rectangle? ....

c) What is the area of the shape below? ....

6 cm

11 cm

Problem Solving

Sometimes you will not be given all the lengths of a shape, but you will always be able to work them out by looking at the lengths you are given and calculating the difference. In this shape, length a must be $10\,cm - 4\,cm = 6\,cm$.

4 cm

a

10 cm

Score: _____ / 3

Challenge 3

Fill in the spaces in this table for these different quadrilaterals:

Width	Length	Perimeter	Area
20 cm	20 cm		400 cm²
15 cm	25 cm	80 cm	
		60 cm	200 cm²
100 cm		500 cm	

Challenge 4

Look at this shape:

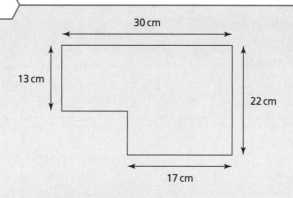

Problem Solving

If you are given a seemingly complicated shape to calculate the area for, simply divide it into simpler shapes like squares and rectangles. Work out the individual areas for those shapes and then add them together.

a) Calculate the perimeter of the shape. ....

b) Calculate the area of the shape. ....

Now Try This!

1. Steve is working with a square that has a perimeter of 60 cm.
   Donna is working with a square that has double the width of Steve's square.
   What is the area of Donna's square?

   A 225 cm²   **B** 150 cm²   **C** 300 cm²   **D** 900 cm²   **E** 700 cm²

2. Look at this triangle:

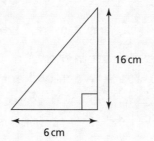

   What is the area of the triangle?

   A 48 cm²   **B** 96 cm²   **C** 20 cm²   **D** 40 cm²   **E** 64 cm²

Total score _____ / 16

LOW   CONFIDENCE   HIGH

Geometry

Let's Get S-t-r-e-t-c-h-i-n-g!

Geometry is working with shapes and understanding them. It involves identifying shapes and angles. The edge of a 3D shape is where two sides meet. The vertex (plural: vertices) is where two edges meet (in other words, a corner).

Make sure you know how many faces, edges and vertices these 3D shapes have: square-based pyramid; cone; cylinder; sphere; hemisphere; triangular prism; cube; cuboid.

Challenge 1

a) I am looking at an equilateral triangle.

What is the size of each of the individual angles? ....

b) Find the size of angle x in this triangle:

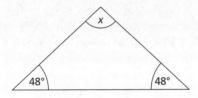

....

c) What type of triangle is the one shown above? ....

Score: _____ / 3

Challenge 2

a) This triangle is connected to a straight line.

Find the size of angle x in this triangle. ....

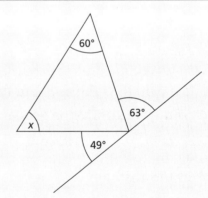

b) This square has been cut in half by a line that goes from the top left corner to the bottom right corner to create two new shapes.

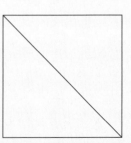

What is the sum of the angles in one of those shapes? ....

Score: _____ / 2

Challenge 3

a) Plot the coordinates C (3, 6) and D (6, 6) on the grid to make a square.

b) Translate the square by (3, 3).

   What are the new coordinates of point C? ....

c) Plot the point E at (5, 0) to make the triangle ABE. Now draw a horizontal line from (0, 3) to (9, 3).

d) Reflect the triangle ABE in the horizontal line.

   What are the new coordinates of point E after the reflection? ....

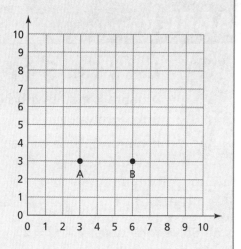

Score: _____ / 4

Challenge 4

a) Which 3D shape has 4 triangular faces, 1 square face, 8 edges and 5 vertices?

   ....

b) Which 3D shape has 2 faces, 1 edge and 1 vertex?

   ....

Score: _____ / 2

Now Try This!

1. Robert is working on an isosceles triangle.
   He notes that the size of the largest angle is 70 degrees.
   What is the size of one of the other angles?

   A 100 degrees   **B** 70 degrees   **C** 40 degrees   **D** 55 degrees   **E** 60 degrees

2. Paula is working with a circle that has a radius of 50 cm.
   Jack is working with a circle that is twice the diameter of Paula's circle.
   The circle Dave is working on has a radius the same size as the diameter of Jack's circle.
   What is the diameter of Dave's circle?

   A 50 cm   **B** 200 cm   **C** 100 cm   **D** 400 cm   **E** 250 cm

Score: _____ / 2

Total score _____ / 13

LOW   CONFIDENCE   HIGH

Let's Get S-t-r-e-t-c-h-i-n-g!

Algebra is maths with symbols instead of numbers. It helps us to find unknown values.

If $y + 4 = 6$, then we can work out that $y = 2$.

Challenge 1

a) Solve for y when $y + 12 = 25$

$y =$ _____

b) Find x when $5x = 25$

$x =$ _____

c) Find x when $9x - 63 = 0$

$x =$ _____

d) Find y when $\dfrac{125}{y} = 25$

$y =$ _____

e) Find y when $12y - 6 = 10y$

$y =$ _____

f) Find x when $30x + 300 = x + 590$

$x =$ _____

Score: _____ / 6

Challenge 2

If $x = 6$, find y when:

a) $5x + y = 38$

$y =$ _____

b) $15x = 4y + 72$

$y =$ _____

If $y = 8$, find x when:

c) $5y + 7 = 26 + x$

$x =$ _____

d) $(7 + y) - x = 1$

$x =$ _____

If $x = -4$, find y when:

e) $2x = -10 + y$

$y =$ _____

f) $-15 - x = -16 - y$

$y =$ _____

Problem Solving

Remember to solve equations by moving values either side of the equals sign. So if, for example, you have a +25 to the left of the equals sign, you can move it to the right and it becomes −25. You are doing the same thing to both sides of the equation (subtracting 25). This method will help you to break down and solve the more difficult algebraic equations.

Score: _____ / 6

Challenge 3

a) Solve x when:

$9x - 30 = 2x + 19$

$x =$ _____

b) Solve y when:

$14y^2 = 56$

$y =$ _____

c) Solve x when:

$\frac{50}{x} = 2x$

$x =$ _____

d) Solve y when:

$35y^2 = 35$

$y =$ _____

Challenge 4

Find the value of y if x = 2 in these equations:

a) $3 + 2x(y + 1) = 27$

$y =$ _____

b) $29 + 3x(y + 7) = 77$

$y =$ _____

Find the value of y if x = 9 in these equations:

c) $16x + 16 + 9y = 190 - y$

$y =$ _____

d) $(x^2 + 25) + 2y = 133 - y$

$y =$ _____

Top Tip

Take care when you are multiplying expressions with brackets. For example, $3x(y + 2)$ means you multiply $3x$ by both y and the 2, so you get $3xy + 6x$.

Now Try This!

1. Ahmed is working with this square.
   The square has a width of 6y + 3 cm.

   6y + 3 cm

   What is the perimeter of the square in centimetres?

   A $24y + 6$ **B** $24y + 12$ **C** $12y + 6$ **D** $12y + 12$ **E** $24y + 8$

2. Jenny is working on a rectangle that has a width of 2x + y cm and a length of 7x + 2y cm.
   What is the perimeter of the rectangle in centimetres?

   A $16x + 6y$ **B** $18x + 6y$ **C** $18x + 4y$ **D** $18x + 2y$ **E** $16x + 2y$

Total score _____ /22

LOW   CONFIDENCE   HIGH

Let's Get S-t-r-e-t-c-h-i-n-g!

When you have two unknown values and two equations relating to them, you have simultaneous equations. So if you know that $3x + 2y = 13$ and that $x + 5y = 13$, you can solve to find x and y.

Problem Solving

With simultaneous equations, you need to get yourself in a position where you can find one value. You can do this by getting one of the equations in a form that means you can subtract the other. You can then substitute that value into the original equations to work out the other value.

In the example above left, multiplying the second equation by 3 gives $3x + 15y = 39$. Now you can subtract the first equation to remove the x to obtain $13y = 26$, $y = 2$. Substitute into the original equation: $3x + 2(2) = 13$, $3x + 4 = 13$, $3x = 9$, $x = 3$. So $x = 3$ and $y = 2$.

Challenge 1

a) I buy 4 rubbers and 3 pencils from a shop. The total cost is £2.90.

   If the rubbers are 50p each, how much does one pencil cost? ....

b) At a fast-food stall, I buy 4 hot dogs and 3 hamburgers for a total cost of £12.50.

   Write an expression for x and y, where x is the price of a hot dog and y is the price of a hamburger. ....

c) At another fast-food bar, a customer buys 4 portions of chips and 3 burgers at a total cost of £6.50.

   If a burger costs £1.50, how much is a portion of chips? ....

d) Multiply the equation $9x = 5.50$ by 2. What do you get? ....

Score: _____ / 4

Challenge 2

a) Find y where: $7y + x = 29$

   $x = 15$

   $y = $ ....

b) Find y where: $12y + 2x = 30$

   $x = 9$

   $y = $ ....

c) Find y where: $22y + 4x = 96$

   $x = 13$

   $y = $ ....

d) Find y where: $300 - y - 3x = 90$

   $x = 50$

   $y = $ ....

Score: _____ / 4

Challenge 3

a) Multiply these equations by 2:

  i) $4x + 3y = 2.10$ _____

  ii) $4x + y = 7.25$ _____

b) Multiply these equations by 3:

  i) $5y + 3x = 12$ _____

  ii) $y + 4x = 21$ _____

c) Subtract the bottom equation from the top:

$7y + 3x = 7.50$

$7y + x = 4$

_____

d) Subtract the top equation from the bottom:

$12y + 6x = 27$

$20y + 10x = 45$

_____

Challenge 4

Solve these simultaneous equations for x and y.

a) $4x + 2y = 5$

     $2x + 3y = 3.50$

         $x =$ _____ $y =$ _____

b) $3x + 2y = 4.90$

     $4x + 4y = 8.20$

         $x =$ _____ $y =$ _____

c) $3x + 4y = 8.35$

     $5x + 2y = 7.85$

         $x =$ _____ $y =$ _____

Now Try This!

1. Rick goes to a shop and buys 3 staplers and 4 folders for £8.50.
   His friend goes to the same shop and buys 6 staplers and 5 folders for £14.
   How much does 1 stapler cost in the shop?

   A £1   **B** £1.50   **C** £2   **D** £1.75   **E** 75p

2. In a supermarket, a customer buys 4 kitchen rolls and 3 cheese slices for £4.10.
   Another customer buys 3 kitchen rolls and 6 cheese slices for £5.70.
   How much does 1 kitchen roll cost in the supermarket?

   A 70p   **B** 50p   **C** 40p   **D** 60p   **E** 55p

Total score _____ /22

LOW   CONFIDENCE   HIGH

Let's Get S-t-r-e-t-c-h-i-n-g!

The mean, median, mode and range are values that help us to understand data better:

- The mean is the average value.
- The median is the middle value when the data is ordered.
- The mode is the value that occurs most often.
- The range is the difference between the highest and the lowest values in the data.

Challenge 1

Consider these numbers: | 7 | 14 | 14 | 21 | 4

a) What is the mean of the numbers? ....

b) What is the mode of the numbers? ....

c) What is the range of the numbers? ....

d) What is the median of the numbers? ....

e) Consider the highest number in the list.

What number would you need to change this to
in order to make the new range of the numbers 30? ....

Score: _____ / 5

Challenge 2

Consider these numbers: | 16 | 0 | 0 | 32 | 12 | 6

a) What is the mode of the numbers? ....

b) What is the mean of the numbers? ....

c) What is the median of the numbers? ....

d) What is the range of the numbers? ....

Problem Solving

If you are presented with an even number of values, you find the median by taking the average of the two middle values when the data is arranged in order.

Now add twelve to the highest number in the box and answer these questions:

e) What is the mean of the numbers now? ....

f) What is the range of the numbers now? ....

g) What is the median of the numbers now? ....

Score: _____ / 7

Five friends counted how many stickers they owned and the results are shown in this bar chart:

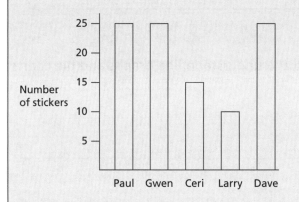

Number of stickers

Paul   Gwen   Ceri   Larry   Dave

Top Tip

You will often be presented with data in graphical form, such as a bar or a pie chart. Work through the chart to reveal the numbers and calculate the mean, median, mode and range from there.

a) What was the mode number of stickers? ....

b) What was the median number of stickers? ....

c) What was the range in the number of stickers? ....

d) What was the mean number of stickers? ....

Score: _____ / 4

Challenge 4

Liv has a set of number cards:

| 3 | 13 | 7 | 3 | 14 |

a) What is the range in the numbers on her cards? ....

b) Add the mode, median and mean numbers of all the cards.

What is the total? ....

Score: _____ / 2

Now Try This!

1. Rhiannon scored 82, 44, 73, 49, 65 and 71 in her first six exams.

   After the seventh and last exam, she had a mean result of 66 across all her exams.

   What score did she get in her last exam?

   A 79 **B** 78 **C** 80 **D** 76 **E** 82

2. The values a, b and c have a mode of 15 and a mean of 13.

   a is the lowest value.

   What is the value of $a + b$?

   A 20 **B** 19 **C** 25 **D** 22 **E** 24

Score: _____ / 2

Total score _____ / 20

LOW   CONFIDENCE   HIGH

Let's Get S-t-r-e-t-c-h-i-n-g!

Statistics questions in the 11+ test will require you to understand line graphs and pie charts and interpret them fully.

Challenge 1

Krishan has plotted the number of achievement points he gained at school each day on this graph.

a) Join up the points to make a line graph.

b) What was the total number of achievement points Krishan got across the three days?

....

c) What was the range in the number of achievement points he got?

....

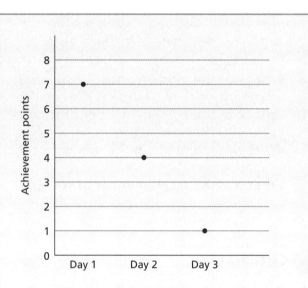

Score: _____ / 3

Challenge 2

Draw a line graph to show this data:

Day	Temperature (°C)
Monday	−3
Tuesday	5
Wednesday	9
Thursday	−2
Friday	2

Score: _____ / 6

Challenge 3

Rowan is using this data table in order to create a pie chart of the colours of pens he owns.
Fill in the gaps in the table.

Colour	Number	Size of pie chart angle
Black	50	90 degrees
Red		
Green		90 degrees

Score: _____ /3

Challenge 4

A group of pupils were asked which sport they played in the summer.
The results are recorded in this pie chart:

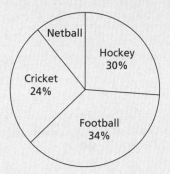

Problem Solving

You could be shown graphs or data that is incomplete. The information provided will always give you the tools to find out the missing data.

a) 96 pupils said they played cricket.

How many pupils said they played netball? ....

b) What was the total number of pupils that were asked? ....

Score: _____ /2

Now Try This!

1. Three-fifths of the people on a train are looking at their phone.

   Of the remainder, one half are reading and the other half are looking out of the window.

   If you were presenting this information in a pie chart, what angle size would you use to represent the people looking out of the window?

   A 60 degrees   B 90 degrees   C 72 degrees   D 75 degrees   E 65 degrees

2. 360 people are not wearing sunglasses. 240 people are wearing sunglasses.

   If you were presenting this information in a pie chart, what angle size would you use to represent the people who are wearing sunglasses?

   A 144 degrees   B 160 degrees   C 180 degrees   D 240 degrees   E 200 degrees

Score: _____ /2

Total score _____ /16

LOW   CONFIDENCE   HIGH

1. a) What is the lowest common multiple of 6 and 8? (1)

    b) What is the highest common factor of 12 and 18? (1)

2. Steve is looking at his train timetable:

Southampton	12:08
London	13:34
Birmingham	15:06
Newcastle	18:02

    a) Steve gets on the train at Southampton and leaves it at London.

        How long does he spend on the train? (1)

    b) Steve's friend gets on the train at Birmingham. However, it suffers a 27-minute delay.

        At what time does his friend arrive at Newcastle? (1)

3. This chart shows how far various towns are from London in miles.

    London

64	Town A		
78	22	Town B	
39	51	63	Town C
46	67	75	36	Town D

    Problem Solving

    Timetables for trains, trams or buses often appear in 11+ test questions. Make sure you can read them and understand any manipulation of the time or places that you are asked about.

    a) Which town is furthest from London? (1)

    b) How far is Town D from Town B? (1)

    c) How much closer is Town B to Town A than Town D is to Town A? (1)

4. Find the next number in each of these sequences.

a)   14, 19, 24, 29, … (1)

_____

b)   32, 29, 25, 20, 14, … (1)

_____

c)   6, 14, 20, 34, 54, … (1)

_____

5. Triangle *ABC* has been plotted on the graph grid below.

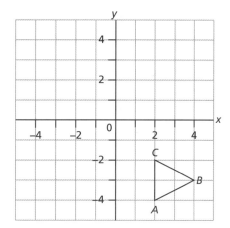

a)   What are the coordinates of point *A*? (1)

(_____ , _____)

b)   Reflect the triangle in the *x* axis.

What are the new coordinates of point *C*? (1)

(_____ , _____)

6. Jessie ran for 36 minutes at 10 kilometres per hour and then for 18 minutes at 5 kilometres per hour.

How far did she run in total? (1)

_____

7. Think about the hands on the face of a clock.

    a) What is the smaller angle between two clock hands at 4:00? (1)

    _____

    b) What is the angle between two clock hands at 2:30?
    Think about where the hour hand will be. (1)

    _____

8. Triangle ABC has been drawn on the graph grid below.

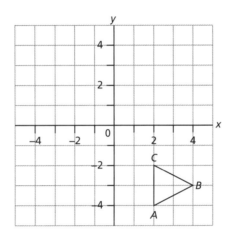

    a) Translate the triangle by (1, 4).

    What are the new coordinates of point B? (1)

    (_____ , _____)

    b) Using the graph above, draw a diagonal line where x = y.
    Reflect the original triangle in this line.

    What are the new coordinates of point C? (1)

    (_____ , _____)

Problem Solving

With coordinates questions, make sure you know how to translate, reflect and rotate shapes. Reflections can also be through diagonal lines.

9. Pawel leaves his house at 8:45 am.
   He travels at an average speed of 5 mph and reaches school at 9:15 am.

   How far is it from Pawel's house to his school? (1)

   _____

10. Annabelle is tossing a fair coin.

    What is the probability that it lands on the Heads side three times in a row?
    Give your answer as a fraction. (1)

    ....

11. Give all your answers as percentages.

    Mushy writes all the numbers from 1–20 on 20 different number cards.
    He then puts the cards in a bag.

    a) If he picks out one card at random, what is the probability it will be an odd number? (1)

        ....

    b) What is the probability that Mushy will pull out a number that is a factor of 5? (1)

        ....

    c) What is the probability that Mushy will not pull out a square number? (1)

        ....

    d) What is the probability that Mushy will pull out a prime number? (1)

        ....

12. Think about the points of a compass.

    a) Angelique is facing due West. She turns by 180 degrees anticlockwise.

        In which direction is she now facing? (1)

        ....

    b) Adil is facing exactly South East. He turns by 90 degrees clockwise.

        In which direction is he now facing? (1)

        ....

Top Tip

Learn all the points of a compass and at what angle they are pointing. There are lots of mnemonics for remembering these. For example: Never Eat Soggy Waffles!

Total score _____ /25

LOW   CONFIDENCE   HIGH

Let's Get S-t-r-e-t-c-h-i-n-g!

An author might use several different techniques to create a particular atmosphere. In 11+ comprehension questions, you are often asked to consider:

- what type of atmosphere has been created
- how that atmosphere has been created
- how a setting or the author's choice of language can contribute in creating a particular feeling or response in a reader.

Top Tip

In literature, an atmosphere generally means a feeling or mood created by the words of the story. Authors work hard to create and sustain an appropriate atmosphere because the reader is much more likely to feel immersed in the narrative if there is a convincing atmosphere which provokes a feeling.

Challenge 1

Read the extract and answer the questions that follow on a separate piece of paper.

On his way to the station William remembered with a fresh pang of disappointment that he was taking nothing down to the kiddies. Poor little chaps! It was hard lines on them. Their first words always were as they ran to greet him, "What have you got for me, Daddy?" and he had nothing. He would have to buy them some sweets at the station. But that was what he had done for the past four Saturdays; their faces had fallen last time when they saw the same old boxes produced again.

And Paddy had said, "I had red ribbing on mine *bee*-fore!"

And Johnny had said, "It's always pink on mine. I hate pink."

But what was William to do? The affair wasn't so easily settled. In the old days, of course, he would have taken a taxi off to a decent toyshop and chosen them something in five minutes.

From *Marriage à la Mode*, by Katherine Mansfield

a) What atmosphere has the writer created in this extract? (3)

b) How does this contrast with what we might expect when children are bought sweets? (2)

c) What do you think William means by 'the affair wasn't so easily settled'? (2)

Score: _____ /7

Challenge 2

Read the extract and answer the questions that follow on a separate piece of paper.

Top Tip

Think about how **you** feel when you read a story. What effect does the setting, tone and mood have on you as a reader? When you write a story yourself, try to create a particular atmosphere in order to make your reader feel a certain way.

Problem Solving

Comprehension texts will sometimes be chosen from books written many years ago. Therefore the sentence structure may be different to what you are used to. Part of the test is whether you can unpick the meaning of what you read.

LETTER I.

To Mrs. Saville, England.

St. Petersburgh, Dec. 11th, 17–.

You will rejoice to hear that no disaster has accompanied the commencement of an enterprise which you have regarded with such evil forebodings. I arrived here yesterday; and my first task is to assure my dear sister of my welfare, and increasing confidence in the success of my undertaking.

I am already far north of London; and as I walk in the streets of Petersburgh, I feel a cold northern breeze play upon my cheeks, which braces my nerves, and fills me with delight. Do you understand this feeling? This breeze, which has travelled from the regions towards which I am advancing, gives me a foretaste of those icy climes. Inspirited by this wind of promise, my day dreams become more fervent and vivid. I try in vain to be persuaded that the pole is the seat of frost and desolation; it ever presents itself to my imagination as the region of beauty and delight. There, Margaret, the sun is forever visible, its broad disk just skirting the horizon, and diffusing a perpetual splendour. There – for with your leave, my sister, I will put some trust in preceding navigators – there snow and frost are banished; and, sailing over a calm sea, we may be wafted to a land surpassing in wonders and in beauty every region hitherto discovered on the habitable globe. Its productions and features may be without example, as the phenomena of the heavenly bodies undoubtedly are in those undiscovered solitudes. What may not be expected in a country of eternal light?

From *Frankenstein*; or, *The Modern Prometheus*, by Mary Shelley

a) How does the recipient of the letter feel that things will go? (2)

b) What is the recipient's full name? (1)

c) How does the writer of the letter feel that things are going? Use your own words to explain. (2)

d) Where has the writer gone? (1)

e) How does the writer feel about the weather? Give evidence to support your answer. (2)

f) 'I try in vain to be persuaded that the pole is the seat of frost and desolation; it ever presents itself to my imagination as the region of beauty and delight.' What does the writer mean by this? (3)

g) Who are 'preceding navigators'? (1)

h) What atmosphere is created in the extract? Support your answer with evidence from the text. (6)

Score: _____ / 18

> **Now Try This!**

Read the extract and select the correct answer to the question.

The intense interest aroused in the public by what was known at the time as "The Styles Case" has now somewhat subsided. Nevertheless, in view of the world-wide notoriety which attended it, I have been asked, both by my friend Poirot and the family themselves, to write an account of the whole story. This, we trust, will effectually silence the sensational rumours which still persist.

From *The Mysterious Affair at Styles*, by Agatha Christie

What do we learn of "The Styles Case" in this extract?

A It is an exciting piece of fiction.
B Members of the public have made up their own minds.
C There is much scandal as it is a tantalising story.
D The case follows a great detective.

Top Tip

Description of the setting and of *how* the characters speak or move is often crucial in establishing the tone and atmosphere of an extract.

Score: _____ / 1

Total score _____ / 26

LOW CONFIDENCE HIGH

Let's Get S-t-r-e-t-c-h-i-n-g!

The characters are often vital to our enjoyment of literature. Remember to think about why characters are behaving in a particular way. Think about them as people with real opinions, feelings and responses.

Challenge 1

Read the extract and then answer the questions on a separate piece of paper.
In this extract, Dorian Grey is looking at the portrait of himself which seems to have supernatural powers. Since it was painted, instead of the beautiful Dorian ageing, the figure in the portrait seems to be getting older in his place every time he commits a bad deed.

But the picture? What was he to say of that? It held the secret of his life, and told his story. It had taught him to love his own beauty. Would it teach him to loathe his own soul? Would he ever look at it again?

No; it was merely an illusion wrought on the troubled senses. The horrible night that he had passed had left phantoms behind it. Suddenly there had fallen upon his brain that tiny scarlet speck that makes men mad. The picture had not changed. It was folly to think so.

Yet it was watching him, with its beautiful marred face and its cruel smile. Its bright hair gleamed in the early sunlight. Its blue eyes met his own. A sense of infinite pity, not for himself, but for the painted image of himself, came over him. It had altered already, and would alter more. Its gold would wither into grey. Its red and white roses would die. For every sin that he committed, a stain would fleck and wreck its fairness. But he would not sin. The picture, changed or unchanged, would be to him the visible emblem of conscience. He would resist temptation. He would not see Lord Henry any more—would not, at any rate, listen to those subtle poisonous theories that in Basil Hallward's garden had first stirred within him the passion for impossible things. He would go back to Sibyl Vane, make her amends, marry her, try to love her again. Yes, it was his duty to do so. She must have suffered more than he had. [...] He had been selfish and cruel to her. The fascination that she had exercised over him would return. They would be happy together. His life with her would be beautiful and pure.

He got up from his chair and drew a large screen right in front of the portrait, shuddering as he glanced at it. "How horrible!" he murmured to himself, and he walked across to the window and opened it. When he stepped out on to the grass, he drew a deep breath. The fresh morning air seemed to drive away all his sombre passions. He thought only of Sibyl. A faint echo of his love came back to him. He repeated her name over and over again. The birds that were singing in the dew-drenched garden seemed to be telling the flowers about her.

From The Picture of Dorian Grey, by Oscar Wilde

a) What does the author mean when Dorian asks of the picture: 'Would it teach him to loathe his own soul?'? (2)

b) What technique does the writer use when he says 'Yet [the picture] was watching him'? What effect does this create? (2)

c) In your own words, explain what Dorian feels when he thinks about Sybil Vane. (3)

d) How does the weather and natural world mimic what Dorian feels? (2)

Score: _____ /9

Think about three memorable characters in any texts you have read.

Draw three mind maps on a separate piece of paper to show what makes them memorable. Is it the dialogue? Is it their quirky personality? Are they likeable? Try to think of key moments in the literature that make the character seem realistic and rounded.

Top Tip

Talking of someone's 'quirks' refers to the little unusual details of their personality.

Score: _____ / 15

Challenge 3

Read the extract and answer the questions that follow on a separate piece of paper.

It was there that, several years ago, I saw him for the first time; and the sight pulled me up sharp. Even then he was the most striking figure in Starkfield, though he was but the ruin of a man. It was not so much his great height that marked him, for the "natives" were easily singled out by their lank longitude from the stockier foreign breed: it was the careless powerful look he had, in spite of a lameness checking each step like the jerk of a chain. There was something bleak and unapproachable in his face, and he was so stiffened and grizzled that I took him for an old man and was surprised to hear that he was not more than fifty-two. I had this from Harmon Gow, who had driven the stage from Bettsbridge to Starkfield in pre-trolley days and knew the chronicle of all the families on his line.

From *Ethan Frome*, by Edith Wharton

a) What does the narrator mean when he says, 'the sight pulled me up sharp'? (2)

b) List, in as much detail as possible, what we learn of the man's appearance in the passage. Give a wide range of points and use your own words where you can. (6)

c) Physically, what are the local people in Starkfield like? (1)

d) i) Identify a simile used in the passage. (1)   ii) What is the effect of this comparison? (2)

Score: _____ / 12

Now Try This!

Read the extract below and select the correct answer to the question.

One of my most vivid memories is of coming back West from prep school and later from college at Christmas time. Those who went farther than Chicago would gather in the old dim Union Station at six o'clock of a December evening, with a few Chicago friends, already caught up into their own holiday gaieties, to bid them a hasty goodbye. I remember the fur coats of the girls returning from Miss This-or-That's and the chatter of frozen breath and the hands waving overhead as we caught sight of old acquaintances, and the matchings of invitations: "Are you going to the Ordways'? the Herseys'? the Schultzes'?" and the long green tickets clasped tight in our gloved hands. And last the murky yellow cars of the Chicago, Milwaukee and St. Paul railroad looking cheerful as Christmas itself on the tracks beside the gate.

From *The Great Gatsby*, by F Scott Fitzgerald

"Are you going to the Ordways'? the Herseys'? the Schultzes'?"
What effect does the writer's use of the hosts' names create in this extract?

A   All of the hosts appear anonymous and homogenous.

B   Each host seems extremely important and individual.

C   The parties seem more extravagant due to the names being given.

D   The narrator seems envious because the names are of important people.

Score: _____ / 1

Total score _____ / 37

LOW   CONFIDENCE   HIGH

Verbal Ability

37

Inference, Deduction and Rhetorical Devices

Let's Get S-t-r-e-t-c-h-i-n-g!

When you read, look out for rhetorical devices and literary techniques used to create a particular atmosphere or a specific effect. Sometimes you will need to 'read between the lines' and deduce information about the story, rather than just answering fact-finding questions. Try to:

- think about what the author is saying in greater depth
- question how characters think and feel
- look out for dramatic irony (where the reader knows more than the characters).

Top Tip

Make sure you can identify and define these literary devices:

- Simile
- Personification
- Metaphor
- Alliteration
- Onomatopoeia
- Vivid imagery

Challenge 1

Read the following poem and then answer the questions on a separate piece of paper.

By The Sea

I started early, took my dog,
And visited the sea;
The mermaids in the basement
Came out to look at me,

And frigates in the upper floor
Extended hempen hands,
Presuming me to be a mouse
Aground, upon the sands.

But no man moved me till the tide
Went past my simple shoe,
And past my apron and my belt,
And past my bodice too,

And made as he would eat me up
As wholly as a dew
Upon a dandelion's sleeve —
And then I started too.

And he — he followed close behind;
I felt his silver heel
Upon my ankle, — then my shoes
Would overflow with pearl.

Until we met the solid town,
No man he seemed to know;
And bowing with a mighty look
At me, the sea withdrew.

by Emily Dickinson

* frigates = warships
* hempen = made out of hemp (rough plant-based) fibres

a) Re-read the first stanza. What technique does the writer use when she says, 'The mermaids in the basement / Came out to look at me,'?
What effect does this create? (3)

b) What technique does the writer use when she says, 'Extended hempen hands,'?
What effect does this create? (3)

c) What technique does the writer use at the beginning of lines 3 and 4 in stanza 3?
What effect does this create? (3)

d) What technique does the writer use when she says, 'And bowing with a mighty look / At me, the sea withdrew'?
What effect does this create? (3)

Score: _____ / 12

Challenge 2

Read the extract and answer the questions that follow on a separate piece of paper.

The little old town of Mayenfeld is charmingly situated. From it a footpath leads through green, well-wooded stretches to the foot of the heights which look down imposingly upon the valley. Where the footpath begins to go steeply and abruptly up the Alps, the heath, with its short grass and pungent herbage, at once sends out its soft perfume to meet the wayfarer.

One bright sunny morning in June, a tall, vigorous maiden of the mountain region climbed up the narrow path, leading a little girl by the hand. The youngster's cheeks were in such a glow that it showed even through her sun-browned skin. Small wonder though! for in spite of the heat, the little one, who was scarcely five years old, was bundled up as if she had to brave a bitter frost. Her shape was difficult to distinguish, for she wore two dresses, if not three, and around her shoulders a large red cotton shawl. With her feet encased in heavy hob-nailed boots, this hot and shapeless little person toiled up the mountain.

The pair had been climbing for about an hour when they reached a hamlet half-way up the great mountain named the Alm. It was the elder girl's home town, and therefore she was greeted from nearly every house; [...]

There a few cottages lay scattered about, from the furthest of which a voice called out to her through an open door: "Deta, please wait one moment! I am coming with you, if you are going further up." [...]

A stout, pleasant-looking woman stepped out of the house and joined the two.

"Where are you taking the child, Deta?" asked the newcomer. "Is she the child your sister left?"

"Yes," Deta assured her; "I am taking her up to the Alm-Uncle and there I want her to remain."

"You can't really mean to take her there Deta. You must have lost your senses, to go to him. I am sure the old man will show you the door and won't even listen to what you say."

"Why not? As he's her grandfather, it is high time he should do something for the child. I have taken care of her until this summer and now a good place has been offered to me. The child shall not hinder me from accepting it, I tell you that!"

"It would not be so hard, if he were like other mortals. But you know him yourself. How could he *look* after a child, especially such a little one? She'll never get along with him, I am sure of that!—But tell me of your prospects."

"I am going to a splendid house in Frankfurt. Last summer some people went off to the baths and I took care of their rooms. As they got to like me, they wanted to take me along, but I could not leave. They have come back now and have persuaded me to go with them."

From *Heidi*, by Joanna Spyri

a) What impressions are we given of the setting in the first paragraph? (3)

b) Using your own words, what do we learn about the little girl in the second paragraph? (5)

c) Re-read the paragraph starting 'It would not be so hard'. What is implied about Alm-Uncle? (2)

d) What does the newcomer mean when she says 'But tell me of your prospects'? (1)

e) What job is Deta going to do? Use your own words. (2)

Score: _____ / 13

> **Now Try This!**

Read the extract below and select the correct answer to the question.

As he was sitting at breakfast next morning, Basil Hallward was shown into the room.
"I am so glad I have found you, Dorian," he said gravely. "I called last night, and they told me you were at the opera. Of course, I knew that was impossible. But I wish you had left word where you had really gone to. I passed a dreadful evening, half afraid that one tragedy might be followed by another. I think you might have telegraphed for me when you heard of it first. I read of it quite by chance in a late edition of *The Globe* that I picked up at the club. I came here at once and was miserable at not finding you. I can't tell you how heart-broken I am about the whole thing. I know what you must suffer. But where were you?"

From *The Picture of Dorian Gray,* by Oscar Wilde

What do we learn about Dorian in the extract?

A He is a thespian.

B He is elusive and secretive.

C He makes others happy with his presence.

D It is possible to read of his exploits in the paper.

Score: _____ / 1

Total score _____ / 26

LOW   CONFIDENCE   HIGH

Let's Get S-t-r-e-t-c-h-i-n-g!

Sharp spelling skills will serve you well in your 11+ test. Be prepared to identify a wrongly spelt word or find the correct prefix for a given word. Take particular care with homophones – these are words that sound the same but have different meanings.

Top Tip
If there is an 'ee' sound after the letter 'c', the digraph 'ei' is usually used.

Challenge 1

Complete each word with the correct spelling for the answer to each given clue. Each answer is a word with the 'ei' or 'ie' digraph.

a) Shows proof you have paid for something   r _ _ _ _ _ _

b) Give way to something   y _ _ _ _

c) Aggressive   f _ _ _ _ _

d) A pale brown colour   b _ _ _ _

Top Tip
The digraphs 'ei' and 'ie' can be used for different sounds, e.g. 'ee', 'ay', 'i' and 'ih'.

Score: _____ / 4

Challenge 2

Add a prefix to each word below to form its antonym (opposite meaning).

a) __practical

b) __resolute

c) __definite

d) __compose

e) __even

f) __respective

g) ___trust

h) __legal

Top Tip
If the root word starts with 'm' or 'p', the prefix 'im' is usually used.

Top Tip
If the root word starts with 'l', use the prefix 'il'.
If the root word starts with 'r', the prefix 'ir' is generally used.

Score: _____ / 8

---

a) Underline the correct word in each homophone pair in bold in the sentences below.

   i)   We watched the parade in celebration of the queen's 60-year **reign / rein**.

   ii) I decided to **alter / altar** the annoying ring tone on my new phone.

   iii) After the wild weather, the trees are almost completely **bare / bear**.

   iv) I noticed a degree of **dissent / descent** amongst the members at tonight's meeting.

   v)   Dad helped me **practice / practise** my lines for the school play.

b) Write a near-homophone for each word below.

   i)   addition _____   ii) proceed _____

   iii) accept _____   iv) lightening _____

   v)   access _____   vi) desert _____

Score: _____ /11

Challenge 4

Write the plural form of each singular word.

a) goose _____   b) trout _____   c) diagnosis _____

d) ellipsis _____   e) quiz _____   f) series _____

g) leaf _____   h) ox _____   i) aircraft _____

Score: _____ /9

Now Try This!

1. Select the word below that has been misspelt.

a)

A	B	C	D	E
guarantee	explicit	interruption	correspondant	definition

b)

A	B	C	D	E
rhythmical	embarrassment	conscientious	discrepancy	pyschological

2. Complete the words below by inserting the missing letters.

a) p a r l _ _ m e n t   b) d e s p _ r _ t e

c) n _ _ s a n c e   d) p r i v _ l _ g e

Score: _____ /6

Total score _____ /38

LOW   CONFIDENCE   HIGH

Let's Get S-t-r-e-t-c-h-i-n-g!

Make sure your grammar skills are up to scratch for the 11+ test. You might be asked to identify the word class of a particular word, so make sure you know what is meant by a common noun, proper noun, abstract noun, concrete noun, verb, adjective, adverb, pronoun, preposition and determiner. You could also be asked to select correct verb forms or identify punctuation mistakes within a sentence.

Top Tip

The subject in a sentence is the person, animal or thing that is carrying out the action, shown by the verb. The verb tells you what the subject is 'doing', 'being' or 'having'.

Top Tip

The subject in a sentence can be a noun, proper noun, pronoun or noun phrase.

Challenge 1

Underline the subject in each sentence below. Write **N**, **PN**, **P** or **NP** on the line to indicate whether you have underlined a noun (N), proper noun (PN), pronoun (P) or noun phrase (NP).

a) Buckingham Palace is one of London's most popular tourist attractions. ....

b) The amazing acrobats thrilled us with their breathtaking acts. ....

c) Looking around him, he was certain he'd been here before. ....

d) "Please will you call an electrician?" ....

e) Hailstones pounded the caravan roof as we cooked our breakfast. ....

Score: _____ / 5

Top Tip

The subjunctive mood can be used when expressing a wish, an emotion, possibility, or an action that has not yet occurred. It is often used in a subordinate clause, e.g. If I *were* you, I'd be careful walking along the cliff path.

Challenge 2

Insert the correct form of the verb 'be' so that it agrees with the subject of each sentence.

a) A group of Year 6 children .... representing the school at the debate.

b) Mum said me and my sister .... allowed to go into town on our bikes tomorrow.

c) If I .... to win a million pounds, I'd cruise around the Caribbean.

d) Should you .... cold, please turn on the heating.

Score: _____ / 4

Challenge 3

Rewrite the passage below, putting any verbs that are in the wrong tense in the correct tense.

A few years ago, we decide to go camping. It is our first time and I must say, we are very excited. Little do we know that it is going to rain the entire time! However, I wouldn't say it ruins our trip – we are able to spend the evenings in the recreation room where we play table tennis and meet lots of new friends. We also swim in the lake and build dens in the forest.

....

....

....

....

....

....

Score: _____ /11

Challenge 4

Read these two sentences.

Last night, Matt saw his dad **on** TV. He **was** being interviewed about the incredible **discovery** of **ancient** gold coins which **he** found in the garden.

Write the underlined words in the correct column of the table according to their word class.

Noun	Adjective	Verb	Adverbial phrase	Preposition	Pronoun

Score: _____ /6

Now Try This!

1. Select the word that is a pronoun.

A	B	C	D	E
hers	her	who	that	mine

2. What type of word is 'very'?

A	B	C	D	E
verb	preposition	adverb	noun	determiner

3. What type of word is 'clueless'?

A	B	C	D	E
adverb	noun	pronoun	verb	adjective

Score: _____ /3

Total score _____ / 29

LOW   CONFIDENCE   HIGH

Verbal Ability   43

Word Definitions

Let's Get S-t-r-e-t-c-h-i-n-g!

You will be tested on your knowledge of the meaning of words. You can improve your skills in this area by writing down any unfamiliar words you come across while reading. Look up their definitions in a dictionary and make a note of them. However, remember that some words can have more than one meaning, depending on the context in which they are used.

Top Tip

You can sometimes work out the meaning of unfamiliar words by the context of the sentence in which they appear.

Challenge 1

Use a dictionary to find the meaning of each word then write a sentence containing the word.

Word	Meaning	Word in a sentence
clemency		
gregarious		
meticulous		
wholesome		

Score: _____ / 8

Challenge 2

Each incomplete word on the right has a similar meaning to the word on the left.
Fill in the missing letters in each word on the right.

a) scour   s _ _ _ b

b) expect   a n _ _ c _ p a _ _

c) extra   s _ p e _ f l _ o _ _

d) unconventional   u _ o _ t _ o _ o x

Score: _____ / 4

Challenge 3

Underline the two words, one from each group, that are closest in meaning.

a) (plaster build wound)   (clock gash bricks)

b) (subterfuge profanity scripture)   (trick loyalty subterrain)

c) (painstaking placid obstinate)   (meticulous slapdash excruciating)

d) (abstain adhere dissolve)   (disappear liquify bind)

Score: _____ / 4

Challenge 4

Draw a line to match each word on the left with its correct definition on the right.

	A period of one hundred years
sentry	Describes an anti-viral medicine
	A soldier who guards something
	Mean and nasty
innocuous	An event thought to tell what will happen in the future
	Something that is harmless
meagre	The final word of a prayer
	A score of one hundred runs in cricket
omen	A very small amount / not enough of something
	A religious leader

Score: _____ / 4

Now Try This!

Read the sentence in bold and then select the most appropriate word to answer each question.

The accomplished gymnast seemed to defy the laws of gravity.

1. What does the word 'accomplished' mean?

A	B	C	D	E
flexible	famous	clever	skilled	unpolished

2. What does the word 'defy' mean?

A	B	C	D	E
encourage	disobey	honour	reflect	defeat

Score: _____ / 2

Total score _____ / 22

LOW   CONFIDENCE   HIGH

Odd One Out

Let's Get S-t-r-e-t-c-h-i-n-g!

Your knowledge of the meanings of words could be tested with questions that ask you to identify one word, or two words, that are the odd ones out within a group.

Problem Solving

Watch out for words that belong to more than one word class or have more than one meaning. These could be the key to solving the question.

Challenge 1

Write a sentence containing each word below, showing their two different meanings.

a) saw ....

b) saw ....

c) clog ....

d) clog ....

e) career ....

f) career ....

Score: _____ / 6

Challenge 2

The odd one out in each set of emboldened words is the one that completes the sentence. Underline that word.

a) Robert **strolled / rushed / ambled / sauntered** to the front door when he heard the urgent ring of the doorbell.

b) The secret agent managed to **activate / launch / immobilise / discharge** the missile and avoid an international crisis.

c) In my project about amphibians, I included the life cycle of **butterflies / bees / spiders / frogs**.

d) **Somalia / Oceania / Africa / Asia** is one of 13 countries that the Equator passes through.

Score: _____ / 4

Underline the odd one out in each group of words.

a) coal   kindling   firewood   timber

b) mine   yours   theirs   ours

c) seek   search   excavate   discover

d) submerge   quarry   secrete   conceal

e) Choosing from your answers in parts a) to d), identify the word that is the odd one out of the four.

_____

Score: _____ / 5

Top Tip

Watch out for homophones – words that sound the same but have a different meaning and spelling.

Challenge 4

For each set of five words, choose the answer option where both words do not fit with the others.

a) through   thorough   beside   below   though

   A through beside   B beside below   C through below   D thorough though

b) bridal   bridle   isle   groom   usher

   A bridal groom   B bridle isle   C isle usher   D bridal isle

c) promote   bank   back   deposit   sponsor

   A promote back   B back sponsor   C bank deposit   D promote sponsor

Score: _____ / 3

Now Try This!

In each set, four of the words are related in some way. Select the word that does not go with the other four.

1.

A	B	C	D	E
conceive	bewilder	confuse	baffle	befuddle

2.

A	B	C	D	E
bee	beetle	fly	ant	centipede

3.

A	B	C	D	E
sun	star	comet	zodiac	galaxy

Score: _____ / 3

Total score _____ / 21

LOW   CONFIDENCE   HIGH

Let's Get S-t-r-e-t-c-h-i-n-g!

You could be asked to identify a word that has the same or a very similar meaning to another word. These kinds of words are called **synonyms**.

Alternatively, you could be asked to identify a word that is opposite in meaning to another word. These kinds of words are called **antonyms**.

Top Tip

A thesaurus is a good place to look up synonyms. A thesaurus will sometimes provide antonyms too.

Challenge 1

Write two sentences for each word in the table below. One sentence should show the word being used as a noun and the other sentence should show it being used as a verb.

	A sentence that uses the word as a noun	A sentence that uses the word as a verb
bark		
address		
stem		

Score: _____ / 6

Challenge 2

Problem Solving

Always consider any alternative meanings of any words you are given.

a) Underline the **two words** in the sentence that are antonyms.

As the troops approached the besieged city, the panicked inhabitants retreated into their homes.

b) Underline the **two words** in the sentence that are synonyms.

The silversmith expertly fashioned a delicate flower pendant, with exceptionally fragile petals.

c) Complete each word in the sentences below with a word opposite in meaning to the clue.

i) Haleema was **o** _ _ _ _ _ _ _ _ _ _ about the weather.   (Clue: pessimistic)

ii) Finn thought the film's ending was rather **b** _ _ _ _ _ **e**.   (Clue: usual)

Score: _____ / 4

Challenge 3

Underline the **two words**, one from each set of brackets, that are most opposite in meaning.

a) (dissent   altercation   subordination)   (discord   acceptance   refusal)

b) (attraction   fascination   adoration)   (disinterest   disappointment   sadness)

c) (whisper   secrete   divulge)   (sigh   misplace   expose)

d) (superior   sufficient   humble)   (interior   subordinate   exterior)

Score: _____ / 4

Challenge 4

Write four sentences using one word from each box in each sentence. The word you choose from the first two boxes should be related in the same way as the words you choose from the last two boxes.

fragile contract ample resolute	is to	shrink determined plenty robust	as	meagre timid shrivel faint	is to	diminish fainthearted strong insufficient

a) _____ is to _____ as _____ is to _____ .

b) _____ is to _____ as _____ is to _____ .

c) _____ is to _____ as _____ is to _____ .

d) _____ is to _____ as _____ is to _____ .

Score: _____ / 4

Problem Solving

The pair of words you identify as being synonyms (or antonyms) should belong to the same word class.

Now Try This!

1. Select the word from the table that is most similar in meaning to the given word.

   thrash

A	B	C	D	E
push	flog	crash	snap	crush

2. Select the word from the table that is most opposite in meaning to the given word.

   resilient

A	B	C	D	E
desperate	careful	vulnerable	cautious	different

Score: _____ / 2

Total score _____ / 20

LOW   CONFIDENCE   HIGH

Verbal Ability   49

Let's Get S-t-r-e-t-c-h-i-n-g!

You may need to identify a word from a group of five that best corresponds to a given word. These questions test your vocabulary, understanding of language and general knowledge.

Top Tip

Brush up on your knowledge of common expressions and idioms to help you answer word association question types. A dictionary of idioms will help you.

Challenge 1

Insert the missing words to complete the idioms below.

a) A blessing in _____.

b) Barking up the wrong _____.

c) Better late than _____.

d) _____ of a feather flock together.

e) A _____ in time saves nine.

f) A _____ for your thoughts.

Top Tip

Write down as many other idioms as you can. Here are some examples to get you started:

• as clean as a whistle
• it's a piece of cake
• it's raining cats and dogs.

Score: _____ / 6

Challenge 2

Underline the **two words** in each group that are most closely related.

a)	cave	join	excavate	seam	fabric
b)	light	desk	screen	wire	monitor
c)	wrist	ear	nose	knee	head
d)	moon	Earth	asteroid	Jupiter	star

Score: _____ / 4

Top Tip

Reading extensively and listening to news programmes and documentaries can help you expand your vocabulary base, general knowledge and understanding of language.

Challenge 3

Draw lines to match each word on the left to its two meanings on the right.

ornate	determined
	famous
intent	give or offer
	decorative
prominent	aim
	intricate
tender	noticeable
	gentle

Score: _____ / 4

Challenge 4

Underline the word on the right that you would associate with both word pairs on the left.

a) | shape   condition | nation   country | reign regular state kingdom land

b) | oven   cooker | extent   amount | range grill excess simmer temperature

c) | film   play | shape   mould | act cast stage show character

d) | approximate estimated | stormy   wild | inaccurate bleak harsh severe rough

Score: _____ / 4

Now Try This!

Select the word from the table that is most closely associated with the given word.

1. **caution**

A	B	C	D	E
hail	sunshine	rain	cloud	wind

2. **blue**

A	B	C	D	E
sad	happy	funny	angry	nervous

3. **orate**

A	B	C	D	E
hear	view	watch	listen	speak

Score: _____ / 3

Total score _____ / 21

LOW CONFIDENCE HIGH

Let's Get S-t-r-e-t-c-h-i-n-g!

Cloze questions require you to find the missing words in a sentence or a short passage. In other types of cloze questions, you may need to identify the missing letters in an incomplete word.

Problem Solving

The context of the sentence or passage will help you select the correct letters or words.

Challenge 1

Select the appropriate pair of words that completes each sentence below.

a) With no time to (lose, waist, leave), Bethan hurriedly put pressure on the wound (though, while, since) she dialled 999.

   A lose, though   **B** lose, while   **C** waist, while   **D** waist, since   **E** leave, since

b) The late Mohammad Ali (has been, was, will be) one of the greatest boxers of (any, all, every) time.

   A has been, any   **B** has been, all   **C** was, all   **D** was, any   **E** will be, all

c) (In view of, In spite, Despite) the torrential rain, the pilot approached the runway (in, under, with) confidence and landed safely.

   A In view of, in   **B** In spite, under   **C** In spite, with   **D** Despite, in   **E** Despite, with

d) Most of the country is (with, at, of) risk of snow or hail this week as temperatures will (ease, struggle, begin) to rise above 4°C, even in the south.

   A with, ease   **B** with, struggle   **C** at, ease   **D** at, struggle   **E** of, begin

Score: _____ / 4

Challenge 2

Underline the correct word from those in bold to complete each sentence.

a) Martin Luther King was an African American Baptist minister who led the American civil rights movement from 1955 until he was brutally **disintegrated** /**assassinated** / **demoted** in 1968.

b) Some words have letters that are **unpronounced** / **unnecessary** / **undefined**; for example, *cemetery, desperate, different* and *evening*.

c) Vitamin C is well known for being a **portent** / **impotent** / **potent** antioxidant and for its positive effects on our skin and immune function.

d) Rain is the result of water vapour condensing and **participating** / **precipitating** / **permeating**, before falling to the ground under gravity.

Score: _____ / 4

Read the passage and choose the words from the list of options to fill each gap.
Write the letter for each word in the spaces.

A	B	C	D	E	F
frightened	by	confront	has	activity	cooling

G	H	I	J	K	L
inching	intense	up	stepping	natural	successive

The Giant's Causeway on the Antrim coast of Northern Ireland was formed around 60 million years ago, during the Paleogene Period. It was an area of _____ volcanic _____ which resulted in _____ flows of lava _____ toward the coast and _____ when they reached the Atlantic Ocean.

The Giant's Causeway is made _____ of around 40,000 basalt columns tumbling down to the sea. These hexagonal-shaped _____ stones in an area of stunning _____ beauty attract thousands of tourists every year.

Legend _____ it that the Giant's Causeway was built _____ the Irish giant, Finn MacCool, as a crossing to _____ his Scottish rival, the giant Benandonner. Arriving in Ireland for the fight, Benandonner was so _____ at the sight of the massive Irish giant that he ran back to Scotland, ripping up the stones as he went.

Score: _____ / 12

For each space in the passage below (marked Question 1, Question 2, etc.) choose the letter for the correct set of words to fill the gap. Write the letter in the answer spaces below.

"Hold your noise!" cried a terrible voice, as a man [Question 1]. "Keep still, you little devil, or I'll cut your throat!"

A fearful man, [Question 2] with a great iron on his leg. A man with no hat, and with broken shoes, and [Question 3]. A man who had been soaked in water, and smothered in mud, and lamed by stones, and cut by flints, and stung by nettles, and torn by briars; [Question 4] and whose teeth [Question 5] as he seized me by the chin.

A	chattered in his head
B	who limped, and shivered, and glared and growled;
C	with an old rag tied round his head
D	started up from among the graves at the side of the church porch
E	all in coarse grey,

Question 1: _____ Question 2: _____ Question 3: _____ Question 4: _____ Question 5: _____

Score: _____ / 5

Total score _____ / 25

LOW   CONFIDENCE   HIGH

Shuffled Sentences

Let's Get S-t-r-e-t-c-h-i-n-g!

In shuffled sentence questions, you need to re-order sentences where the words have been jumbled up. Then you must identify one word in the sentence that is unnecessary.

Problem Solving

The unnecessary word could be difficult to identify but the answer options will help to narrow down the possibilities for you.

> ### Challenge 1

Solve the clues to complete the crossword. All the answers are homophones.

[Crossword grid with clue numbers: ¹ i, ² v, ⁴ d, ³ t, ⁵ v, ⁶ b, ⁷ a, ⁸ b, ⁹ t]

Problem Solving

In 11+ test questions, you might find that the unnecessary word is one of a pair of homophones.

Across

4. The climb down.
7. A narrow passage between chairs.
8. A type of wild pig.
9. Thick, rubber ring on outside of a wheel.

Down

1. Another word for an island.
2. A tube that carries blood to the heart.
3. To start to feel a lack in energy.
4. A difference of opinion.
5. Interested in your own appearance.
6. To make a hole in something with a tool.

Score: _____ / 10

> ### Challenge 2

Find a subject, verb, adjective, noun and adverb in each sentence below. Write the words in the correct column of the table. There may be more than one of each in each sentence.

a) The vet treated the injured rabbit then returned it carefully to its owner.

b) Forgetful though he is, Val always remembers Vikrum's birthday.

c) We are lucky that our caring teachers work hard to deliver excellent lessons.

d) Ethan has no idea that his older cousin is coming to surprise him later.

Top Tip

Find the subject of the sentence, then pair it with a verb.

Top Tip

If there is an adjective in the sentence, find the subject or noun that it modifies. If there is an adverb, find the verb that it modifies.

Subject	Verb	Adjective	Noun	Adverb

Score: _____ / 5

Write the words in each sentence in the correct order.

a) night a Saturday, have on usually we takeaway

_____

b) comedies and shows watching likes my quiz mum

_____

c) turned frog the prince a an of blink into the eye, was in

_____

d) fonder heart makes the grow absence

_____

Score: _____ / 4

Challenge 4

The words in the sentences of this passage have been shuffled. There is an extra word (or words) in each sentence that does not belong. Rewrite the passage, rearranging the words correctly, and find the words that do not belong.

since been it's grandparents has such saw a long time we our. which the live sea on the small coast view in a cottage has a safe they of the. is my gran an artist paint she encourages and me to she. I the I through to another the door key to her walk studio transported to when am world!

_____

_____

_____

_____

The words that do not belong form a shuffled sentence. Write the sentence correctly on this line.

_____

Score: _____ / 4

Now Try This!

The following sentences are shuffled and contain one unnecessary word. Identify that word.

1. ball in net the post put the striker the.

A	B	C	D	E
net	the	striker	post	in

2. coast flooding east havoc has on caused raining the.

A	B	C	D	E
east	raining	on	has	havoc

3. a can't by it judge cover you book its.

A	B	C	D	E
a	can't	it	book	judge

Score: _____ / 3

Total score _____ / 26

LOW   CONFIDENCE   HIGH

Read this passage carefully, then answer questions 1–14.

Far From the Madding Crowd

by Thomas Hardy

> *In the story, we are introduced to a character called Gabriel Oak.*

DESCRIPTION OF FARMER OAK—AN INCIDENT

1   When Farmer Oak smiled, the corners of his mouth spread till they were within an unimportant distance of his ears, his eyes were reduced to mere chinks, and diverging wrinkles appeared round them, extending upon his countenance like the rays in a rudimentary sketch of the rising sun.

…

  Since he lived six times as many working-days as Sundays, Oak's appearance in his old clothes
5 was most peculiarly his own—the mental picture formed by his neighbours always presenting him as dressed in that way when their imaginations answered to the thought "Gabriel Oak." He wore a low-crowned felt hat, spread out at the base by tight jamming upon the head for security in high winds, and a coat like Dr. Johnson's; his lower extremities being encased in ordinary leather leggings and boots emphatically large, affording to each foot a roomy apartment so constructed
10 that any wearer might stand in a river all day long and know nothing about it—their maker being a conscientious man who always endeavoured to compensate for any weakness in his cut by unstinted dimension and solidity.

  Mr. Oak carried about him, by way of watch, what may be called a small silver clock; in other words, it was a watch as to shape and intention, and a small clock as to size. This instrument being
15 several years older than Oak's grandfather, had the peculiarity of going either too fast or not at all. The smaller of its hands, too, occasionally slipped round on the pivot, and thus, though the minutes were told with precision, nobody could be quite certain of the hour they belonged to. The stopping peculiarity of his watch Oak remedied by thumps and shakes, when it always went on again immediately, and he escaped any evil consequences from the other two defects by constant
20 comparisons with and observations of the sun and stars, and by pressing his face close to the glass of his neighbours' windows when passing their houses, till he could discern the hour marked by the green-faced timekeepers within. It may be mentioned that Oak's fob being difficult of access, by reason of its somewhat high situation in the waistband of his trousers (which also lay at a remote height under his waistcoat), the watch was as a necessity pulled out by throwing the body
25 extremely to one side, compressing the mouth and face to a mere mass of ruddy flesh on account of the exertion required, and drawing up the watch by its chain, like a bucket from a well.

  But some thoughtful persons, who had seen him walking across one of his fields on a certain December morning—sunny and exceedingly mild—might have regarded Gabriel Oak in other aspects than these. In his face one might notice that many of the hues and curves of youth had
30 tarried on to manhood: there even remained in his remoter crannies some relics of the boy. His height and breadth would have been sufficient to make his presence imposing, had they been exhibited with due consideration.

1. What is suggested about Farmer Oak in the first paragraph?   (1)

    A   He is extremely cheerful all the time
    B   He does not often smile
    C   When he is happy, the emotion overtakes his whole visage
    D   He is a very old man and his face reflects this

2. What is Farmer Oak's working pattern?   (1)

    A   He works on Sundays
    B   He works from Monday to Friday each week
    C   He works from Monday to Saturday each week
    D   We are not told clearly in the passage

3. How is Gabriel dressed overall?   (1)

    A   He is dressed in the same way his neighbours always imagine him
    B   He is smartly dressed for Sundays
    C   He is wearing fine clothes made with good quality materials
    D   He is wearing clothes suitable for being outside in all weathers

4. What are 'lower extremities' (line 8)?   (1)

    A   Part of the landscape
    B   Legs and feet
    C   Feet
    D   Ankles

5. How would Gabriel's shoes best be described?   (1)

    A   They are practical, substantial and solidly made
    B   They are the size of houses
    C   His shoes are exquisitely cut and made by a skilled craftsman
    D   They are made of ordinary leather

6. Re-read the paragraph beginning on line 13, 'Mr. Oak carried about him, by way of watch...'
    What does this suggest about the watch?   (1)

    A   Sometimes the watch tells the minutes inaccurately
    B   It is cumbersome, unwieldy and inaccurate
    C   It is precise and accurate despite being an antique
    D   He has inherited the watch from his ancestors

7. What do we learn about Gabriel's approach to timekeeping? (1)

   A   He uses the natural world, his watch and other people's clocks to tell the time
   B   He does not care what time it is as it is too difficult to get his watch out
   C   He uses only the natural world and other people's clocks to tell the time
   D   He is frequently frustrated with his watch

8. Re-read the sentence starting 'It may be mentioned that Oak's fob...' (lines 22–26)
   What technique has been used at the end of the sentence? (1)

   A   Metaphor   B   Simile   C   Alliteration   D   Onomatopoeia

9. 'In his face one might notice that many of the hues and curves of youth had tarried on to manhood: there even remained in his remoter crannies some relics of the boy.' (lines 29–30)
   What does this sentence suggest about Gabriel? (1)

   A   He looks very young for his age
   B   He is fresh-faced and has a youthfulness to his figure
   C   He looks older than his years
   D   His boyish figure is long gone

10. 'His height and breadth would have been sufficient to make his presence imposing, had they been exhibited with due consideration.' (lines 30–32)
    What do we learn about Gabriel in this sentence? (1)

    A   He is always considerate of other people
    B   He often puts people off by using his large size to dominate them
    C   He is tall but not broad but is able to appear frightening and powerful
    D   He is physically large and could appear daunting if he wanted to

11. What type of word is 'extremities' (line 8)? (1)

    A   Pronoun   B   Noun   C   Adjective   D   Adverb

12. What does the word 'discern' (line 21) mean? (1)

    A   Believe   B   Concede   C   Perceive   D   Know

13. What does the word 'regarded' (line 28) mean? (1)

    A   Noted   B   Debated   C   Known   D   Considered

14. What type of word is 'remoter' (line 30)? (1)

    A   Adjective   B   Noun   C   Pronoun   D   Determiner

Questions 15–26 focus on word choice skills.

15. The lines in this poem extract have been shuffled and there is an extra word in each that does not belong. Write the rearranged lines below and write the words that do not belong on the lines to the right. **(4)**

> and to the free Owl went the sea Pussy-cat
> boat in pea-green beautiful a float,
> plenty take money, they of took and some honey,
> coat up five-pound in wrapped note a.

16. Underline the best option in each set of brackets to correctly complete the sentence. **(2)**

   a) The boxer was helpless against his (ally, adversary, auxiliary) and collapsed in the middle of the (round, ring, square).

   b) (In spite of, Due to, Despite) the impending storm, the explorers decided against an (assent, ascent, accent) of the mountain.

17. Underline the best word in each set of brackets to complete the word connection sentences. **(2)**

   a) Fragile is to (delicate china thin) as unknown is to (night obscure sky).

   b) General is to (specific varied unusual) as insipid is to (bland tasty blurred).

18. Circle the word on the right that you could associate with both word pairs on the left. **(2)**

   a) (find discover)   (stain blemish)   freckle   smudge   spot   see

   b) (use purpose)   (do event)   conference   function   use   party

19. Insert the missing letters to complete the words below. **(4)**

   a) c o _ n c _ l   b) p r o c _ _ u r e   c) c a f f _ _ n e   d) p r e c o c _ _ _ s

20. Insert the missing words to complete the idioms below. (4)

   a) Barking up the _____ tree.

   b) Curiosity _____ the cat.

   c) A bolt from the _____ .

   d) All that _____ is not gold.

21. Circle the word that is the odd one out in each group below. (4)

   a) love   anger   jealousy   fear   hate

   b) calmly   softly   quickly   lovely   quietly

   c) whale   horse   dolphin   vole   chameleon

   d) ludicrous   ridiculous   foolish   farcical   hilarious

22. Underline the two words, one from each group, that are closest in meaning. (2)

   a) (sapphire pewter brass)   (silver gold ruby)

   b) (clever amiable confident)   (genial curt despicable)

23. Complete the passage below by choosing the correct words from the box. (11)

lay	by	shed	at	plantation	hot	pond	cold	lived	stand	shade

While I was young I _____ upon my mother's milk, as I could not eat grass. In the

daytime I ran by her side, and _____ night I _____ down close _____

her. When it was _____ we used to _____ by the _____ in the

_____ of the trees, and when it was _____ we had a nice warm _____

near the _____ .   *(from Black Beauty, by Anna Sewell)*

24. Circle two words in each set that do not belong with the other three.   (2)

a)   dismiss   bag   fire   sack   kindling

b)   ornate   sparse   decorative   meagre   elaborate

25. Read the sentence then answer the questions that follow.   (2)

The weather and our potential excursion by sailboat are inextricably linked.

a)   What does the word 'potential' mean?

    A possible   **B** expected   **C** future   **D** exciting   **E** decisive

b)   What does the word 'inextricably' mean?

    A avoidably   **B** perfectly   **C** inseparably   **D** incredibly   **E** deniably

26. Read the sentences and then answer the questions that follow.   (2)

Next week, we are moving to our new house in the countryside. It will be great to have fresh air after living in the inner city for so long.

a)   What type of word is 'to'?

    A verb   **B** noun   **C** preposition   **D** pronoun   **E** adverb

b)   What type of word is 'inner'?

    A pronoun   **B** adjective   **C** preposition   **D** adverb   **E** noun

Total score _____ **/55**

LOW   CONFIDENCE   HIGH

Let's Get S-t-r-e-t-c-h-i-n-g!

Let's practise identifying relationships between different shapes and figures. You will need to identify a series of similarities and differences to select the best fit for a group or to find an 'odd one out'.

Problem Solving

Think about these features when looking for similarities and differences between images:

- Symmetry
- Shading
- Reflection
- Number
- Angles
- Direction of arrows
- Line type
- Rotation
- Size
- Regular / Irregular shapes
- How shapes overlap or touch

Challenge 1

Look at the figures below. Can you identify what the figures in each set have in common? Draw a further figure for each set that follows the same rules.

a)

b)

c)

Score: _____ / 3

Challenge 2

A B C E H K I T
S B D O M V W

a) Sort the letters into **three** distinct groups using symmetry. What are the rules for grouping them?

_____

_____

b) You may find you have one 'odd one out'. Which letter is it and why?

Score: _____ / 2

Bill has five square fields and five rectangular fields. He wants to subdivide them and he plans some layouts.

A B C D E

F G H I J

a) i) Find a similarity between each of the square fields.

_____

_____

ii) Identify a feature that makes one of the square fields different from all of the others.

_____

b) i) Find a similarity between each of the rectangular fields.

_____

ii) Make a case for three different rectangular fields to be the 'odd one out'.

_____

_____

_____

_____

Score: _____ / 4

Now Try This!

1. Work out what makes the images on the left similar to each other. Then find the image on the right that is most like the images on the left.

a)

   |

    A   B   C   D   E

b)

 |

    A   B   C   D   E

2. Look at each line of five images. Work out which image is most unlike the other four.

a)

   A   B   C   D   E

b)

    A   B   C   D   E

Score: _____ / 4

Total score _____ / 13

LOW   CONFIDENCE   HIGH

Let's Get S-t-r-e-t-c-h-i-n-g!

In the following questions you will need to consider how a figure changes, then apply that rule to other shapes.

Problem Solving

Different parts of each figure will change in different ways.

Challenge 1

Manon has a deep-sea fishing business. She is considering various designs for her new fleet of fishing boats. Look at each pair of boats and help Manon to identify the differences.

a) i) Find one difference in the flags.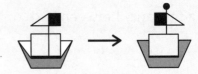

_____

ii) Find two changes in the flagpole.

_____

iii) Find one change in the boat.

_____

b) i) Find one change in the sail.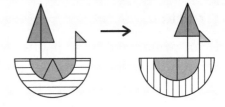

_____

ii) Find two differences in the boat.

_____

c) i) Find one change in the flagpole.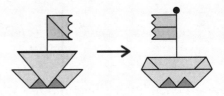

_____

ii) Find three changes in the flag.

_____

_____

iii) Find four changes in the boat.

_____

_____

Score: _____ / 8

Manon also keeps fish in tanks to investigate the best diet for them. Look at how the first fish in each line has changed after its two-week diet, then draw what the third fish will look like when it has changed in the same way.

a)

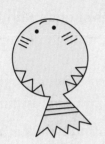  

b)

 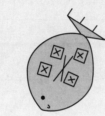 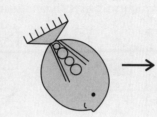

Score: _____ /2

Challenge 3

Finally, Manon turns her attention to her pet goldfish and the coral she grows for them. Look at the first figure in each line and how it changes into the second figure. Then select the correct figure to show how the third image would change in the same way.

a)

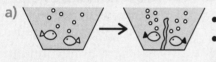 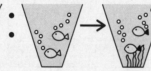

                                        A   B   C   D   E

b)

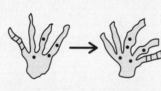   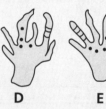

                                          A   B   C   D   E

Score: _____ /2

Now Try This!

Decide which image (A, B, C, D or E) goes with the third image to make a pair like the two on the left.

1.

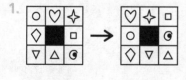

                                          A   B   C   D   E

2.

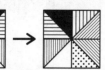

                                          A   B   C   D   E

Score: _____ /2

Total score _____ / 14

LOW   CONFIDENCE   HIGH

Let's Get S-t-r-e-t-c-h-i-n-g!

In the following questions, you will need to think about different types of grids with patterns or shapes in them. Sometimes the patterns flow between the sections of the grid. At other times, there is a rule or change applied.

Challenge 1

Identify the patterns and figures as they change throughout each square grid. Using a ruler where necessary, draw the missing pattern or figure in each section of the grid.

a)

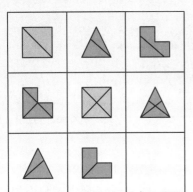

b)

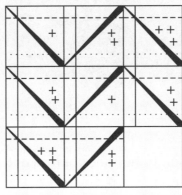

Problem Solving

Look for patterns running horizontally, vertically and diagonally in the square-based, 'complete the grid' questions. When dealing with grids that are not square, patterns can also 'flow' around the edge and run through them.

c)

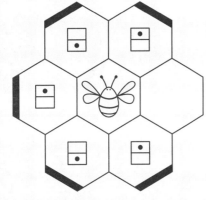

d)

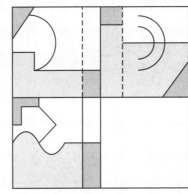

Score: _____ / 4

Challenge 2

Bertie the bee is creating patterns in his honeycomb. Identify how each pattern works. Using a ruler where necessary, draw the missing pattern or figure in the blank section of each grid.

a)

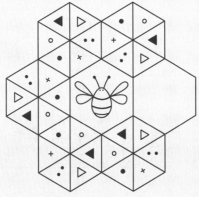

b)

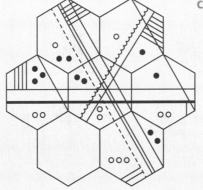

c)

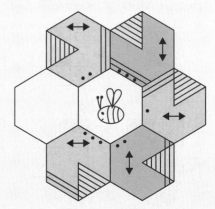

Score: _____ / 3

Bertie tries a new, octagonal honeycomb.
He has left two sections blank. Can you
identify the patterns and complete them?

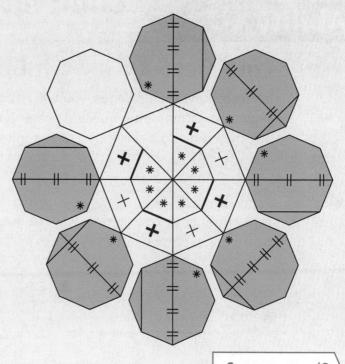

Now Try This!

One of the boxes is empty in the grid on the left. Work out which of the five boxes on the right completes the grid.

1.

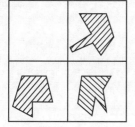

    A   B   C   D   E

2.

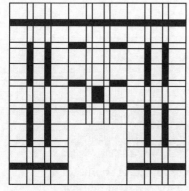

   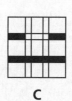   

    A   B   C   D   E

3.

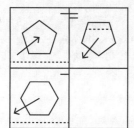

    A   B   C   D   E

Total score _____ /12

LOW   CONFIDENCE   HIGH

Let's Get S-t-r-e-t-c-h-i-n-g!

In the following challenges, you will need to think about how images can alter in a sequence. Often, sequences are presented as a block of five squares in a horizontal row, but they can also be made up of triangles, hexagons or offset squares.

Challenge 1

Look at each sequence below. Identify how each component is changing across the sequence. Are there differences between the top boxes in the sequence compared to the bottom boxes?

a)

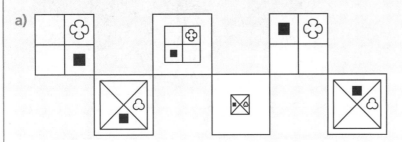

....
....
....
....
....

b)

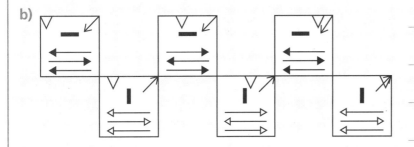

....
....
....
....
....

Score: _____ / 2

Challenge 2

Accurately draw the missing figure in each sequence.
Make sure you include every component in the figure.

a)

b)

c)

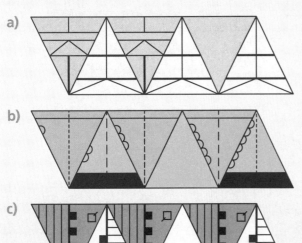

Problem Solving

Sometimes figures alternate between the different boxes in a sequence. At other times, they change in number, orientation or reflection. Different elements of a sequence can change in different ways.

Score: _____ / 3

The hexagonal sequence shown right has several different components:

- The larger circles become increasingly bold working clockwise around the hexagon.
- The crosses alternate between one and two around the hexagon.
- The small circles increase in number (by 1) working clockwise around the hexagon.

Draw your own hexagonal sequences in the shapes below. Remember to include components which change in different ways.

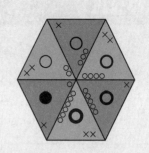

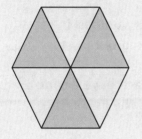 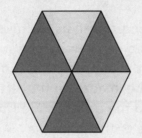 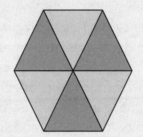

Score: _____ / 3

Now Try This!

Look at the five boxes in each question. One of the boxes is empty. One of the five boxes on the right (A, B, C, D or E) should take the place of the empty one. Decide which one.

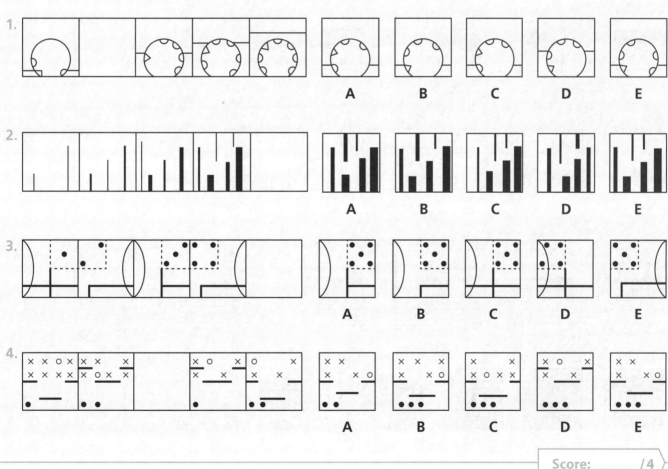

Score: _____ / 4

Total score _____ / 12

Let's Get S-t-r-e-t-c-h-i-n-g!

On the next pages, you will be presented with a different type of challenge: code-breaking. These questions require you to look for similarities in the images with the same code letter, then deduce the correct code for the blank figure on the right-hand side of the question.

Challenge 1

Hugo Hunter runs a detective agency. He has been presented with a new mission: unmasking the thief who has stolen the Clyvedon diamonds. He has asked for your help in solving the mystery. All that remains is a note dropped through Hugo's door on the day after the crime.

To help solve the mystery, look at the following codes. The images on the left each have a code. Work out how the codes go with these images. Then find the correct code from the list on the right that matches the final image on the right-hand side of the question.

As you decode the figures, write the letters in the spaces in the yellow box on page 71, working across the top row first. The top letter of the code for the first figure should be written in the first space in the yellow box, then the bottom letter of the code for the first figure should be written in the second space. The top letter of the code for the second figure should be written in the third space in the yellow box, and so on. Eventually, the letters will spell out a hidden message.

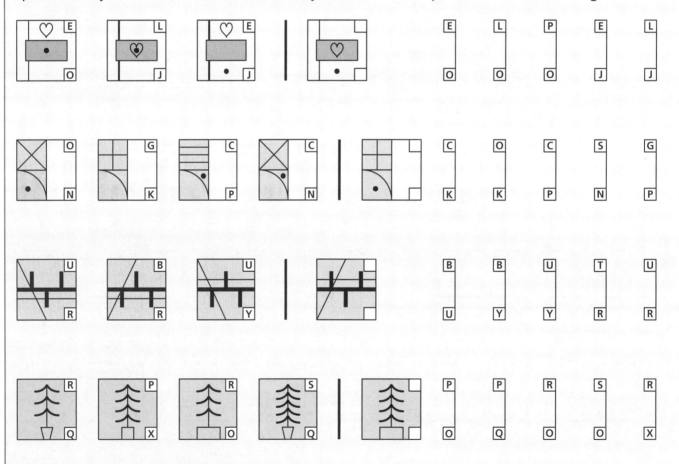

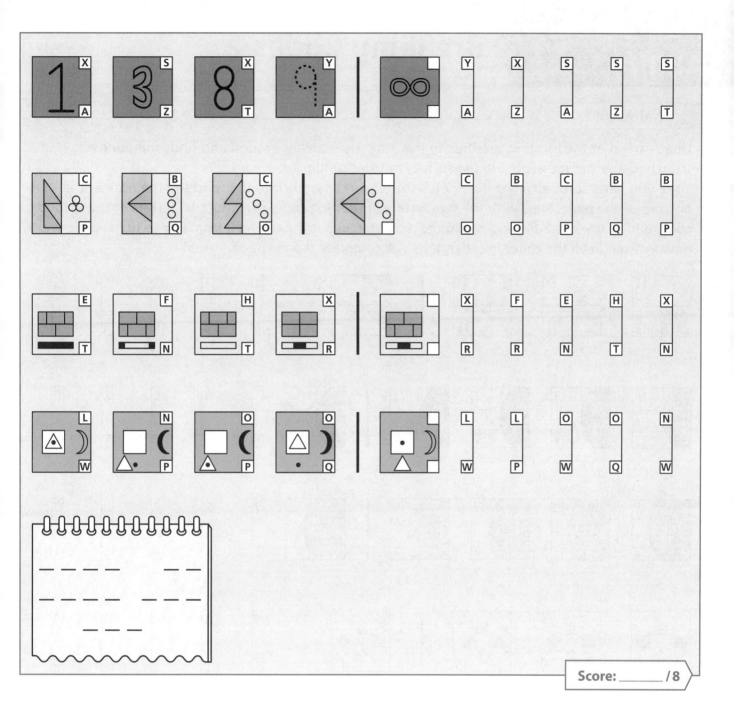

Total score _____ / 8

LOW   CONFIDENCE   HIGH

Score: _____ / 8

Challenge 1

Hugo arrives at the location specified in the note. He searches around and finds someone has scratched another message into the surface in front of him.

Once you have decoded all of the figures, write your answers into the spaces in the note at the bottom of the page. Start with the two letters of the first code, then the two letters of the second code, and so on. Write the codes into the note starting at the top left, from left to right. Once you have written in all the codes in order, they will complete the message.

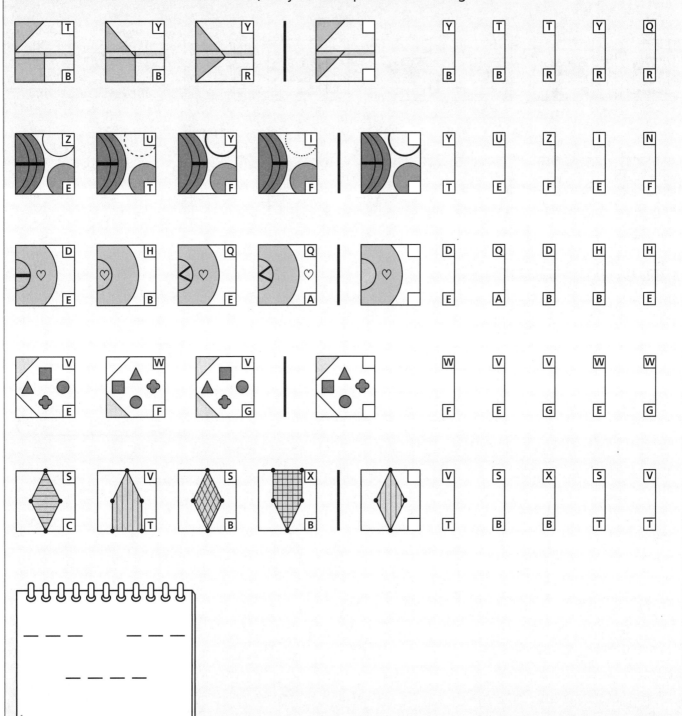

Score: _____ / 5

Hugo follows his compass and arrives at a tree. He can see there is a discarded luggage label at the base of the tree.

To help him identify the name on it, look at the question below. Fit the letters of the correct code onto the luggage label.

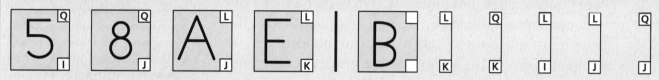

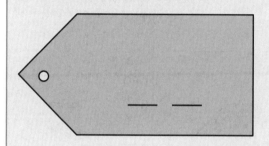

Hugo is pretty sure the culprit is either Light-handed Keith, Quentin Krook, Looter Ingot, Larcenist Jared or Queenie Jailbird.

Who is it according to the luggage label? _____

Score: _____ /2

Total score _____ /7

LOW　CONFIDENCE　HIGH

Let's Get S-t-r-e-t-c-h-i-n-g!

Paper folding questions require you to imagine that a piece of paper has been folded or has had holes punched in it. The hardest questions include holes being punched at different stages of the folding, or using holes of different shapes (such as hearts or hexagons). They might also have different shaped sections folded inwards.

Problem Solving

Some paper folding questions will require you to imagine flaps being folded in on a shape or behind it. Others will require you to imagine a shape cut out of paper is being folded along a given line, so you will need to work out which part of the shape is folded forward.

Challenge 1

In the figures shown right, the front of the paper is coloured blue and the back is coloured orange. Look at how the paper would look if the flap indicated were folded in front and behind.

Draw how the following figures would appear if the flaps indicated were folded behind the paper.

FOLDED IN FRONT →

FOLDED BEHIND →

a)

b)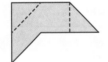

c)

Score: _____ / 3

Challenge 2

Look at the following pieces of paper. The flaps indicated are folded in front of the main shape. Choose how each one would look when the flaps are folded.

a)

A　　B　　C　　D　　E

b)

A　　B　　C　　D　　E

c)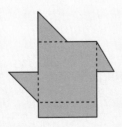

A　　B　　C　　D　　E

Score: _____ / 3

Shown below is a piece of paper with a different colour on each side. Look at how the heart changes position and orientation as the paper is unfolded:

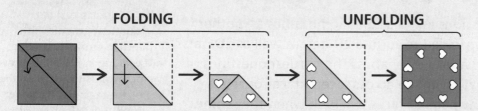

FOLDING   UNFOLDING

Now look at the piece of paper below. Try to draw how the hexagon, pentagon and heart will look at each stage of the paper being unfolded in the last three pieces.

FOLDING   UNFOLDING

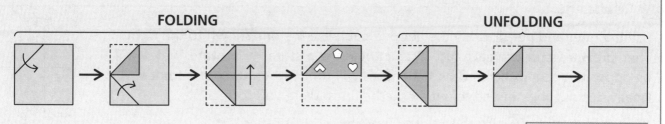

Score: _____ /3

Challenge 4

Look at each piece of paper, which has been folded and has had holes punched through it. On the right, draw what each piece of paper will look like when it is unfolded.

a)

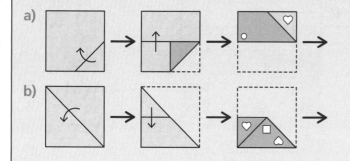

b)

Score: _____ /2

Now Try This!

1. Which answer option shows what the paper would look like when unfolded?

   |

A   B   C   D   E

2. Which answer option shows how each piece of paper would look if folded along the dotted line?

a)

A   B   C   D   E

b)

A   B   C   D   E

Score: _____ /3

Total score _____ / 14

LOW   CONFIDENCE   HIGH

Cubes and Nets

Let's Get S-t-r-e-t-c-h-i-n-g!

Cube and net questions ask you to imagine cubes and other 3D shapes being unfolded to form a 2D net, as well as 2D nets being folded into various 3D shapes. The hardest questions of this kind will repeat an image across several faces or require you to imagine how pairs of faces will look when they come together. Pay close attention to which parts of different figures and shapes will touch, and how they will touch.

Top Tip

For cube and net questions, check which direction arrows and stripes are pointing in. Does the arrow point towards the circle on the net, for example? If so, the arrow will point towards the circle on the cube too.

Challenge 1

Using a ruler and pencil, draw the net of a cube like the one shown to the right. Then draw a picture on each face. Predict how the pictures will rotate, which will be opposite one another and how the faces will touch when the net is folded. Finally, cut out the net and fold it along the lines. Were you correct?

You could do the same for the 10 other possible nets of cubes.

Score: _____ / 1

Challenge 2

For each net, find the pairs of faces which are opposite one another when it is folded into a cube.

a)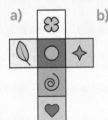
b)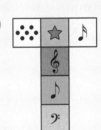
c)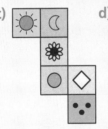
d)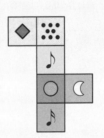
e)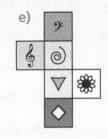
f)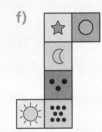

g)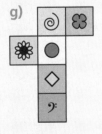
h)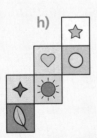
i)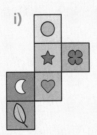
j)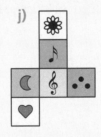
k)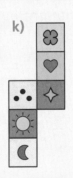

Score: _____ / 11

Challenge 3

a) Circle the four cubes that could be made from the given net.

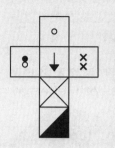

A   B   C   D   E   F   G   H

b) Draw a possible net that would form the 3D shape shown when folded.

i)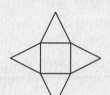

ii)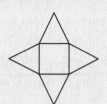

iii)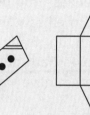

Now Try This!

1. Which net could be folded to make the cube shown?

a)

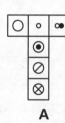 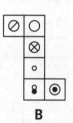 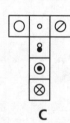  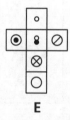

A   B   C   D   E

b)

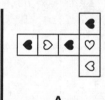 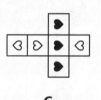 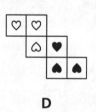 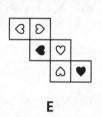

A   B   C   D   E

2. Which cube could be made from the net shown?

a)

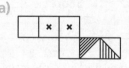

A   B   C   D   E

b)

A   B   C   D   E

Problem Solving

If more than one face has the same pattern, double check which of those faces you need to think about!

Total score _____ /23

LOW   CONFIDENCE   HIGH

Let's Get S-t-r-e-t-c-h-i-n-g!

11+ questions might ask you to imagine that shapes are rotating (turning around a point) or are reflecting as though there is a mirror line. Sometimes shapes can be both reflected and rotated, so look carefully to spot what has happened.

Top Tip

The easiest way to practise these questions is to use tracing paper or acetate to experiment with how figures look when they are reflected and rotated.

Challenge 1

Rachael has a rug business. The profit margin is extremely tight so, to save money, she has asked the weavers to duplicate just one design per rug. On each rug, shade any squares that show **rotations** of the original design in yellow. Shade any squares that show **reflections** of the original design in blue (these have also been rotated at the same time).

a)

b)

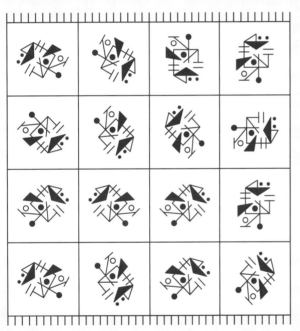

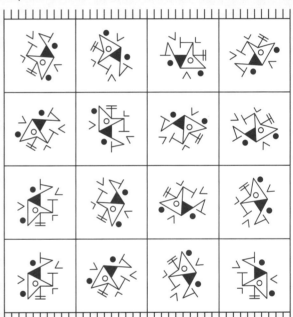

Score: _____ /2

Challenge 2

Rupert has a logo consultancy business. He has a client who wants a logo that will look exactly the same on both sides of her glass door (so it will be identical for the customers entering and exiting the shop without needing to put a copy of the logo on both sides of the door).

Circle the best logo for the client's needs.

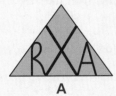

A

B

C

D

E

Score: _____ /1

Octavia's interior design company has been asked to consider some shelf layouts for an important client. She wants to experiment with two different designs. To help her, draw the reflection (in a vertical mirror line) of these shelves.

a)

b)

Score: _____ /2

Now Try This!

Look at the figures on the left-hand side. Select the answer which shows the figure rotated.

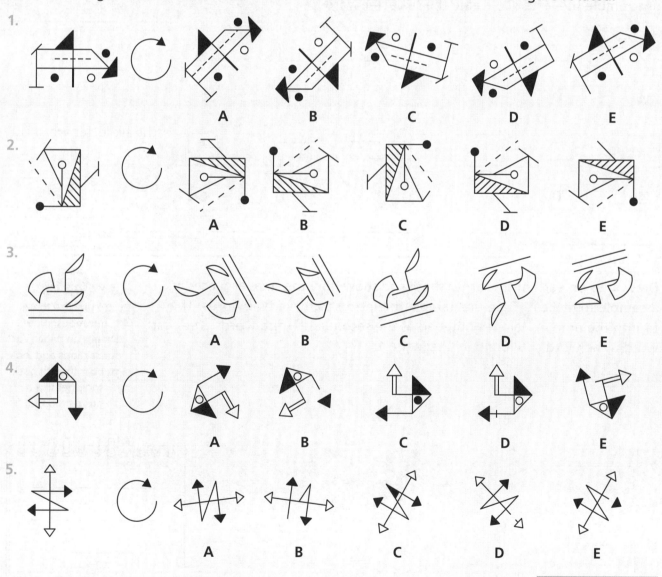

	A	B	C	D	E
1.					
2.					
3.					
4.					
5.					

Score: _____ /5

Total score _____ / 10

LOW   CONFIDENCE   HIGH

Hidden and Composite Shapes

Let's Get S-t-r-e-t-c-h-i-n-g!

Hidden and composite shape questions require you to look for figures hidden in a larger picture, or imagine smaller figures moving to form a larger shape. You will need to visualise the shapes moving and rotating (but not reflecting).

Challenge 1

Horace has been set a secret mission by his boss, Martha. He needs to find the hidden jewels from a recent robbery by solving some clues. In order to understand the first clue, look at the picture on the right.

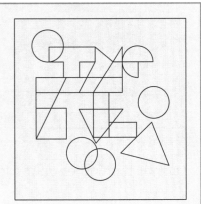

Some of the shapes below are hidden in the picture. They could be rotated but not reflected. Each shape corresponds to a letter of a word you need to find. If a shape appears twice, the letter will be in the word twice. Once you have found all the hidden shapes, unscramble the letters to create the six-letter word.

W   O   U   E   N   L

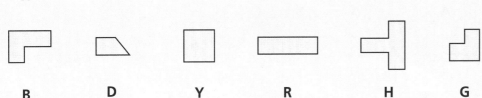

B   D   Y   R   H   G

The six-letter word is:

_ _ _ _ _ _

Score: _____ / 6

Challenge 2

Draw lines on each of the larger shapes to show how the smaller pieces assemble to make it. Then unscramble the letters to make two words. They fit into the note in Horace's notepad as the second and third words. The first word is the word you found in Challenge 1.

Top Tip

To practise these questions, draw shapes on paper, cut out sections and look at how they fit back together like a jigsaw puzzle.

a)

b)

c)

Score: _____ / 4

Challenge 3

Horace's instructions are to meet Martha at the location she has specified at a particular time. Help Horace find the time of the meeting by looking at the following questions. For each figure, look at the shape on the left-hand side. It is hidden in one of the figures on the right-hand side.

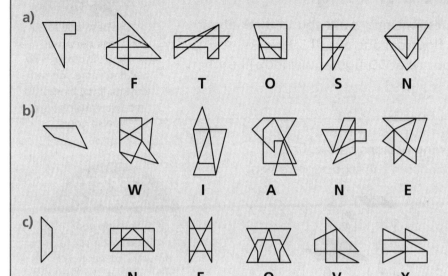

a)   F   T   O   S   N

b)

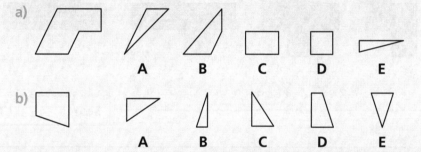

W   I   A   N   E

c)

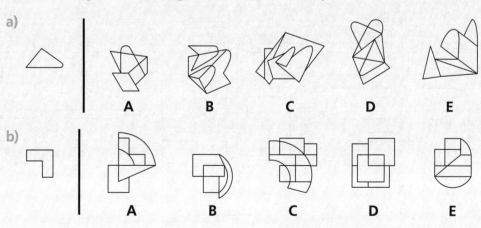

N   E   O   V   X

Write the letters of the correct figures in order to reveal the time of the meeting. _____

Score: _____ /3

Now Try This!

1. Identify which three shapes on the right-hand side can be put together (including rotation, but not reflection) to form the shape on the left-hand side.

a)   A   B   C   D   E

b)   A   B   C   D   E

2. Select the figure on the right which has the shape on the left hidden in it.

a)   A   B   C   D   E

b)   A   B   C   D   E

Score: _____ /4

Total score _____ /17

LOW   CONFIDENCE   HIGH

Let's Get S-t-r-e-t-c-h-i-n-g!

Other spatial reasoning questions might ask you to think about making or deconstructing figures made out of 3D blocks. You might also need to work out what 3D figures will look like when viewed from other angles.

Top Tip

The best way to practise questions involving 3D blocks is by building some yourself with small toy blocks. 3D modelling using junk is also good!

Challenge 1

For each of the three proposed building designs below, find the plan (top-down) view of each one from the six options given.

Problem Solving

To develop your problem solving skills, draw the view of each building from the right-hand side. Work out which building has the smallest area on its right-hand side.

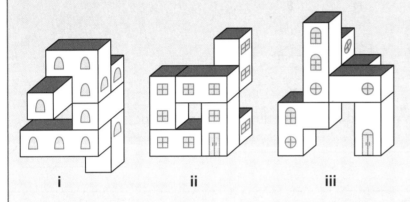

i   ii   iii

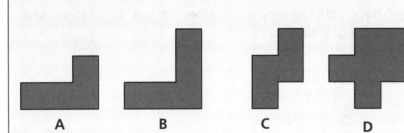

A   B   C   D   E   F

Score: _____ /3

Challenge 2

Find the correct set of blocks to make each building in Challenge 1.

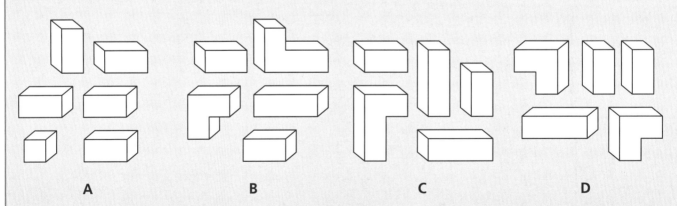

A   B   C   D

Building **i**: ☐   Building **ii**: ☐   Building **iii**: ☐

Score: _____ /3

Challenge 3

Oliver has been playing with his toy bricks.
He has made the following scene.
Draw the plan (top-down) view of each of
the four sets of blocks using the grid below.

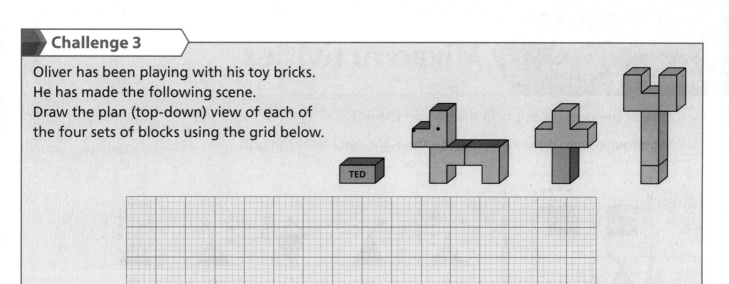

Score: _____ /4

Now Try This!

Which set of blocks (A, B, C, D or E) can be used to create each 3D model?

1.

A

B

C

D

E

2.

A

B

C

D

E

Score: _____ /2

Total score _____ /12

LOW CONFIDENCE HIGH

1. One of the boxes is empty in the grid on the left.

   Work out which of the five boxes on the right completes the grid. (2)

a)

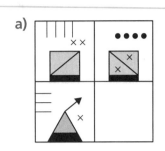

| A | B | C | D | E |

b)

| A | B | C | D | E |

2. There are five boxes arranged in order. One of the boxes is empty.

   One of the five boxes labelled A–E should take the place of the empty one. Decide which one. (2)

a)

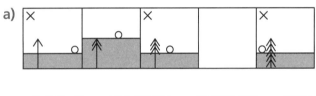

| A | B | C | D | E |

b)

| A | B | C | D | E |

3. The images on the left each have a code. Work out how the codes go with these images. Then look at the image on the right of the vertical line and find its code from the five options given. (2)

a)

    A   B   C   D   E

b)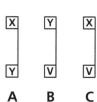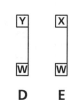

    A   B   C   D   E

4. You are given two figures with an arrow between them. Then there is another figure with an arrow pointing to five more figures labelled A–E. Decide which one of these five figures completes a pair like the two above. (2)

a)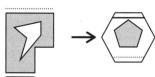

        A   B   C   D   E

b)

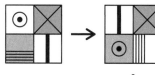

        A   B   C   D   E

5. Work out what makes the two images on the left similar to each other. Then find the image on the right that is most like the two images on the left. (2)

a)

    A   B   C   D   E

b)

    A   B   C   D   E

6. Look at the line of five images. Work out which image is most unlike the other four. (3)

a)

  A   B   C   D   E

b)

  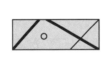  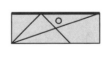

  A   B   C   D   E

c)

  A   B   C   D   E

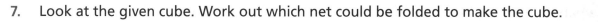
7. Look at the given cube. Work out which net could be folded to make the cube. (2)

a)

 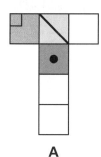 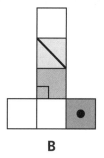 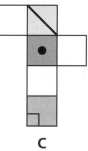 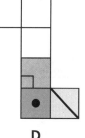 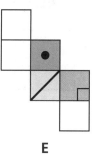

| A | B | C | D | E |

b)

 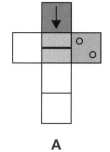 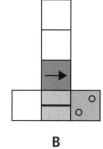 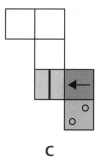 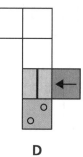 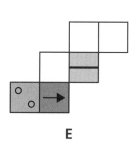

| A | B | C | D | E |

8. Match shapes i, ii and iii to their correct rotations A, B and C. (2)

| i | ii | iii |

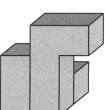 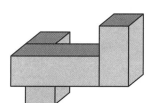 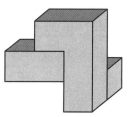

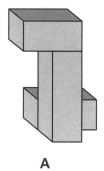 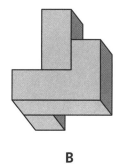 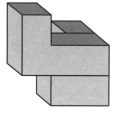

| A | B | C |

9. Look at the paper below, which is folded before holes are punched through it. Which answer option shows what the paper would look like when unfolded? (2)

a)

1 hole punched at this stage

2 holes punched at this stage

A   B   C   D   E

b)

1 hole punched at this stage

2 holes punched at this stage

A   B   C   D   E

Total score _____ **/ 19**

LOW   CONFIDENCE   HIGH

Collins

Test Paper 1

Instructions:

1. Ensure you have pencils and an eraser with you.

2. Make sure you are able to see a clock or watch.

3. Write your name on the answer sheet.

4. Do not start until you are told to do so by an adult.

5. Mark your answers on the answer sheet only.

6. All workings must be completed on a separate piece of paper.

7. You should not use a calculator, dictionary or thesaurus at any point in this paper.

8. Move through the sections as quickly as possible and with care.

9. Follow any instructions on each page.

10. You should mark your answers with a horizontal strike, as shown on the answer sheet.

11. If you want to change your answer, ensure that you rub out your first answer and that your second answer is clearly more visible.

12. You can go back and review any questions that are within the section you are working on only.

SECTION 1: COMPREHENSION

 INSTRUCTIONS

 YOU HAVE 12 MINUTES TO COMPLETE THE FOLLOWING SECTION.

YOU HAVE 14 QUESTIONS TO COMPLETE WITHIN THE TIME GIVEN.

We didn't realise what had happened until we heard a helicopter passing over the roof of our house.

It was an air ambulance and it landed next to the main road. One of our neighbours then told us that there had been a car crash near the corner shop and somebody was seriously injured.

Example i

What landed next to the main road?

A A plane

B A hot-air balloon

C A glider

D A helicopter

The correct answer is **D**. This has already been marked in Example i in Section 1 of Test Paper 1 of your answer sheet on page 171.

Example ii

Who said there had been a car accident?

A A neighbour

B A police officer

C A paramedic

D A shopkeeper

The correct answer is **A**. Mark the answer A in Example ii in Section 1 of Test Paper 1 of your answer sheet on page 171.

Read this passage carefully, then answer the questions.

Anne of Green Gables

by LM Montgomery

> *In the passage, Anne has just arrived at Marilla's house.*

1 Anne dropped on her knees and gazed out into the June morning, her eyes glistening with delight. Oh, wasn't it beautiful? Wasn't it a lovely place? Suppose she wasn't really going to stay here! She would imagine she was. There was scope for imagination here.

A huge cherry-tree grew outside, so close that its boughs tapped against the house, and it was so
5 thick-set with blossoms that hardly a leaf was to be seen. On both sides of the house was a big orchard, one of apple-trees and one of cherry-trees, also showered over with blossoms; and their grass was all sprinkled with dandelions. In the garden below were lilac-trees purple with flowers, and their dizzily sweet fragrance drifted up to the window on the morning wind.

Below the garden a green field lush with clover sloped down to the hollow where the brook ran
10 and where scores of white birches grew, upspringing airily out of an undergrowth suggestive of delightful possibilities in ferns and mosses and woodsy things generally. Beyond it was a hill, green and feathery with spruce and fir; there was a gap in it where the gray gable end of the little house she had seen from the other side of the Lake of Shining Waters was visible.

Off to the left were the big barns and beyond them, away down over green, low-sloping fields, was
15 a sparkling blue glimpse of sea.

Anne's beauty-loving eyes lingered on it all, taking everything greedily in. She had looked on so many unlovely places in her life, poor child; but this was as lovely as anything she had ever dreamed.

She knelt there, lost to everything but the loveliness around her, until she was startled by a hand
20 on her shoulder. Marilla had come in unheard by the small dreamer.

"It's time you were dressed," she said curtly.

Marilla really did not know how to talk to the child, and her uncomfortable ignorance made her crisp and curt when she did not mean to be.

Anne stood up and drew a long breath.

25 "Oh, isn't it wonderful?" she said, waving her hand comprehensively at the good world outside.

CONTINUE WORKING

"It's a big tree," said Marilla, "and it blooms great, but the fruit don't amount to much never – small and wormy."

"Oh, I don't mean just the tree; of course it's lovely – yes, it's *radiantly* lovely – it blooms as if it meant it – but I meant everything, the garden and the orchard and the brook and the woods, the
30 whole big dear world. Don't you feel as if you just loved the world on a morning like this? And I can hear the brook laughing all the way up here. Have you ever noticed what cheerful things brooks are? They're always laughing. Even in winter-time I've heard them under the ice. I'm so glad there's a brook near Green Gables. Perhaps you think it doesn't make any difference to me when you're not going to keep me, but it does. I shall always like to remember that there is a
35 brook at Green Gables even if I never see it again. If there wasn't a brook I'd be *haunted* by the uncomfortable feeling that there ought to be one. I'm not in the depths of despair this morning. I never can be in the morning. Isn't it a splendid thing that there are mornings?"

1 **What types of question are 'Oh, wasn't it beautiful?' and 'Wasn't it a lovely place?'**

A Open   B Rhetorical   C Closed   D Leading

2 **Re-read the first paragraph. Why does the writer structure it in this way?**

A It creates a contrast with Marilla.

B It shows that the narrator has very similar impressions of the surroundings to Anne.

C We can see how Anne is thinking, without explicitly being told that it is her voice.

D The reader won't get bored as the sentences are all punchy and short.

3 **What impressions do we get of Anne's surroundings in paragraphs 2–4?**

A They are unpleasant, so Anne doesn't want to do anything except imagine being there.

B Nature has run wild in the area.

C They are entirely a figment of Anne's imagination.

D They are pleasant, suggesting Anne would love to spend more time there.

4 **What do we learn of Anne in the passage?**

A She is imaginative, optimistic and highly superstitious.

B She is untidy and needs prompting to complete basic tasks in the morning.

C She loves beauty in all forms as she has grown up around examples of the beauty of nature.

D She has had a tough life so far, but has a keen appreciation of aesthetically attractive surroundings.

5 Re-read the paragraph beginning on line 28 'Oh, I don't mean just the tree'.
What do we infer about Anne's perception of her surroundings?

A She is so excited she cannot think clearly.

B She is highly attuned to the detail both now and throughout the changing seasons.

C She is prone to moments of depression and desperation.

D She is deeply superstitious and therefore reads more deeply into what she sees.

6 What technique is used to describe the lilac-trees (lines 7–8)?

A Personification   B Simile   C Metaphor   D Sensory imagery

7 What do we learn about Marilla in the passage?

A She is well-meaning but not articulate and is a practical person.

B She is well-spoken, welcoming and wants to make Anne feel at home.

C Marilla is deeply knowledgeable about the natural world outside and likes to share that.

D She has sole care for the beautiful gardens outside the house that Anne loves.

8 We are told 'the fruit don't amount to much never – small and wormy.' (line 26). What does this mean?

A The tree always fruits reliably.

B The tree does not produce any fruit.

C The fruit sometimes weighs a lot.

D The fruit produced is not very good.

9 We are told that 'scores of white birches grew, upspringing airily' (line 10).
Which of the following is closest in meaning?

A The trees are growing sparsely and quickly.

B It is spring-time so plants are growing rapidly.

C Numerous trees are growing and pushing towards the sky.

D Although it is spring, the trees are not yet growing much.

10 What technique does Anne use when she describes the flow of water in the brook?

A Alliteration

B Personification

C Simile

D Pathetic fallacy

CONTINUE WORKING

11 Which of the following are true, according to the passage?

i   The house likely smells delicious inside.

ii The woodland floor likely has a great spectrum of flora and fauna.

iii There is a stream near the house.

iv Weeds grow on the lawns.

v   The hollow slopes down to the field.

A   All of the above

B   i, iii, iv and v

C   All except iv

D   All except v

12 Line 15 refers to 'a sparkling blue glimpse of sea.'

What part of speech is the word 'sparkling'?

A   Adjective

B   Abstract noun

C   Adverb

D   Concrete noun

13 Line 25 says, 'waving her hand comprehensively at the good world outside.'

What is meant by this?

A   Anne gestures to show that she means everything visible from the window.

B   She waves to show she completely understands what is outside.

C   Anne gestures outside because she thinks it's nice there.

D   She waves at the view.

14 Why does Anne look out of the window 'greedily' (line 16)?

A   She is imagining owning everything she can see.

B   She cannot wait to take in more of her surroundings.

C   She is pretending to be absorbed in what she sees to avoid Marilla's sharp tongue.

D   She doesn't like being inside the house.

SECTION 2: SHUFFLED SENTENCES

 INSTRUCTIONS

 YOU HAVE 7 MINUTES TO COMPLETE THE FOLLOWING SECTION.

YOU HAVE 15 QUESTIONS TO COMPLETE WITHIN THE TIME GIVEN.

Example i

The following sentence is shuffled and also contains one unnecessary word. Rearrange the sentence correctly in order to identify the unnecessary word.

lawnmower cut new grass used with the Dad his.

A	B	C	D	E
lawnmower	used	cut	grass	new

The correct answer is **B**. This has already been marked in Example i in Section 2 of Test Paper 1 of your answer sheet on page 171.

Example ii

The following sentence is shuffled and also contains one unnecessary word. Rearrange the sentence correctly in order to identify the unnecessary word.

day the apple nearby a keeps doctor an away.

A	B	C	D	E
day	apple	keeps	away	nearby

The correct answer is **E**. Mark the answer E in Example ii in Section 2 of Test Paper 1 of your answer sheet on page 171.

Each sentence below is shuffled and also contains one unnecessary word. Rearrange each sentence correctly in order to identify the unnecessary word.

1 tap used a with nail the to hammer in mum.

A	B	C	D	E
to	used	nail	hammer	with

2 beautifully plays rehearsal Harriet piano always the.

A	B	C	D	E
beautifully	plays	rehearsal	piano	the

3 in time his farmer the at brings on cows milking.

A	B	C	D	E
on	the	his	at	time

4 the short scissors has cut too hair my hairdresser.

A	B	C	D	E
short	scissors	cut	the	my

5 his bed off night switches every laptop after Finlay before.

A	B	C	D	E
after	before	bed	every	his

6 you were waterproofs sure wear your trip on make the.

A	B	C	D	E
wear	you	make	were	the

7 fallen snow overnight has in the heavy hills fell.

A	B	C	D	E
fallen	in	fell	has	hills

8 on dropped the some pie the hot kitchen floor Faye.

A	B	C	D	E
kitchen	dropped	hot	on	some

9 the walked the picnic before round in we edge of lake our.

A	B	C	D	E
the	in	round	of	our

10 I of save receipts I tend expensive the purchases always make.

A	B	C	D	E
tend	I	of	always	make

11 likes on to plate Raj tomato his ketchup scrambled put eggs.

A	B	C	D	E
on	his	plate	likes	put

12 nuts robin flies onto the bird a table pecked and flew at the.

A	B	C	D	E
flew	flies	onto	at	table

13 past by the carriages cheered as the royal villagers passed.

A	B	C	D	E
passed	by	royal	past	as

14 café so was food in it the eat couldn't salty the such we.

A	B	C	D	E
eat	so	such	was	it

15 we took lots new of photos I with my away were taken camera while.

A	B	C	D	E
taken	lots	took	of	away

Test Paper 1

SECTION 3: NUMERACY

 INSTRUCTIONS

 YOU HAVE 6 MINUTES TO COMPLETE THE FOLLOWING SECTION.

YOU HAVE 13 QUESTIONS TO COMPLETE WITHIN THE TIME GIVEN.

The questions within this section are not multiple choice. Write the answer to each question on the answer sheet by selecting the correct digits from the columns provided.

Example i

Calculate   34 + 51

The correct answer is **85**. This has already been marked in Example i in Section 3 of Test Paper 1 of your answer sheet on page 171.

Example ii

Calculate   75 ÷ 15

The correct answer is **5**. Mark the answer 05 in Example ii in Section 3 of Test Paper 1 of your answer sheet on page 171. Note that a single-digit answer should be marked with a 0 in the left-hand column.

1   Calculate the answer to the following:

$3 \times 8 - 2$

2   Calculate the answer to the following:

$24 - 6 \div 2$

3   Find the number that completes the sequence in place of the ?

5, 2, 7, 9, 16, ?

4   Find the number that completes the sequence in place of the ?

13, 2, 16, 5, 19, 8, 22, ?

5   Which of these numbers is not exactly divisible by both 6 and 9?

72, 90, 18, 36, 54, 96

6   Which of these numbers is not a factor of 64?

1, 2, 4, 8, 12, 16, 32, 64

7   Calculate the mean of this data:

34, 26, 48, 36

8   Calculate the range of this data:

26, −6, 13, 4, 39

9   Find the mode of this data:

72, 26, 23, 104, 23, 28

10   Calculate the median of this data:

12, 28, 6, 19, 32

11   My grandfather was 62 seven years ago.

How old will he be in four years' time?

12   I left the house at 7:34 am. It took me 17 minutes to walk to the train station, 4 minutes waiting for my train to arrive and then a train journey of 1 hour and 12 minutes to get to my destination.

After how many minutes past 9 am did I get to my destination?

13   Add the fifth prime number to the number of lines of symmetry on an equilateral triangle.

What is the answer?

SECTION 4: PROBLEM SOLVING

 INSTRUCTIONS

YOU HAVE 5 MINUTES TO COMPLETE THE FOLLOWING SECTION.

YOU HAVE 10 QUESTIONS TO COMPLETE WITHIN THE TIME GIVEN.

Example i

I buy one adult ticket and two child tickets for a tram journey. An adult ticket costs £4.30 and a child ticket costs £2.40

How much change do I receive from £10?

A	B	C	D	E
£1.90	£1.30	£3.30	70p	90p

The correct answer is **E**. This has already been marked in Example i in Section 4 of Test Paper 1 of your answer sheet on page 172.

Example ii

There are 30 children in a class. 60% of the children in the class are girls.

How many boys are in the class?

A	B	C	D	E
6	18	8	12	10

The correct answer is **D**. Mark the answer D in Example ii in Section 4 of Test Paper 1 of your answer sheet on page 172.

Calculate the following.

1   Bert got 100 marks in his exam, which was 80%.

How many marks were available in the exam in total?

A	B	C	D	E
115	105	110	125	120

2   What is 20% of a quarter of 200?

A	B	C	D	E
20	10	12	14	16

3   I am thinking of a number. I treble it, then add 24 and halve the result. I end up with 102.

What number was I thinking of originally?

A	B	C	D	E
64	58	62	60	70

4   Ralf has four times as many stickers as Virat. Imran has twice as many stickers as Ralf.

If they have 247 stickers between them, how many stickers does Ralf have?

A	B	C	D	E
76	82	68	72	74

5   The width of a square is 14 cm. The length of a rectangle is 40 cm. The rectangle has a length-to-width ratio of 4 : 1.

What is the difference in area between the square and the rectangle?

A	B	C	D	E
244 cm²	24 cm²	68 cm²	400 cm²	204 cm²

6   The cost of a family going to a cricket match in pounds is $14x + 8y$, where x = the number of adults and y = the number of children.

If a family of 3 adults and 4 children go to the match, how much does it cost them in total?

A	B	C	D	E
£100	£76	£74	£82	£60

CONTINUE WORKING

7   A cube has a volume of 216 cm³.

What is the height of the cube?

A	B	C	D	E
8 cm	16 cm	9 cm	12 cm	6 cm

8   Round 4.2494 to the nearest hundredth and round 6,550 to the nearest 500. Add the two rounded numbers.

What is the answer?

A	B	C	D	E
6,504.25	7,004.25	6,504.24	7,004.24	6,604.25

9   Leo wants to buy a laptop in the sale. It is normally £850 but has been reduced by 20%.

If Leo has saved £250 already, how much more money will he need to buy the laptop at the sale price?

A	B	C	D	E
£680	£430	£700	£450	£350

10   I buy 3 rulers and 4 rubbers at a total cost of £2.70. My friend buys 4 rulers and 2 rubbers at the same shop at a total cost of £2.60.

What is the cost of 1 rubber in the shop?

A	B	C	D	E
40p	25p	20p	30p	35p

SECTION 5: SYNONYMS

 INSTRUCTIONS

 YOU HAVE 10 MINUTES TO COMPLETE THE FOLLOWING SECTION.

YOU HAVE 24 QUESTIONS TO COMPLETE WITHIN THE TIME GIVEN.

Example i

Select the word from the table that is most similar in meaning to the following word:

cram

A	B	C	D	E
enable	pressurise	leave	force	deny

The correct answer is **D**. This has already been marked in Example i in Section 5 of Test Paper 1 of your answer sheet on page 172.

Example ii

Select the word from the table that is most similar in meaning to the following word:

safe

A	B	C	D	E
money	protected	secure	bank	cautious

The correct answer is **C**. Mark the answer C in Example ii in Section 5 of Test Paper 1 of your answer sheet on page 172.

Test Paper 1

In each question, select the word from the table that is most similar in meaning to the word above the table.

1   pry

A	B	C	D	E
fling	disapprove	deny	pursue	inquire

2   meagre

A	B	C	D	E
headache	keen	sufficient	sparse	migrant

3   covet

A	B	C	D	E
envy	hide	sign	dream	despair

4   pretentious

A	B	C	D	E
farcical	hilarious	harassed	grateful	affected

5   list

A	B	C	D	E
erect	shopping	lean	call	prop

6   quarried

A	B	C	D	E
exploded	extracted	exported	expected	expelled

7   rouse

A	B	C	D	E
soothe	calm	restore	wake	beat

8 concede

A	B	C	D	E
admit	permit	believe	conceal	deceive

9 refrain

A	B	C	D	E
confess	abstain	derange	reschedule	reapply

10 innocuous

A	B	C	D	E
harmful	dangerous	infectious	difficult	harmless

11 hostile

A	B	C	D	E
sickly	distant	unfriendly	amicable	personable

12 fluorescent

A	B	C	D	E
flowery	scented	opaque	luminous	dull

13 prophet

A	B	C	D	E
gain	clairvoyant	earnings	magician	wizard

14 ominous

A	B	C	D	E
everybody	joyful	annoying	menacing	spiteful

15 patriotic

A	B	C	D	E
nationalistic	rebellious	decisive	intellectual	stoical

CONTINUE WORKING

16 flag

A	B	C	D	E
wave	pole	tire	erect	sleep

17 noxious

A	B	C	D	E
careful	poisonous	harmless	incapable	easy

18 neutral

A	B	C	D	E
one-sided	obvious	blameless	interfering	impartial

19 launch

A	B	C	D	E
end	begin	finish	report	practise

20 poignant

A	B	C	D	E
sharp	faint	touching	ideal	breathless

21 paparazzi

A	B	C	D	E
photographers	journalists	editors	paperboys	magazines

22 demonstrative

A	B	C	D	E
cool	devilish	monstrous	skilled	affectionate

23 bureau

A	B	C	D	E
money	exchange	foreign	department	government

24 canister

A	B	C	D	E
cone	container	oblong	suitcase	bag

SECTION 6: NON-VERBAL ABILITY

 INSTRUCTIONS

 YOU HAVE 7 MINUTES TO COMPLETE THE FOLLOWING SECTION.

YOU HAVE 13 QUESTIONS TO COMPLETE WITHIN THE TIME GIVEN.

Example i

Look at the cube net below. Select the only cube that could be formed from the net.

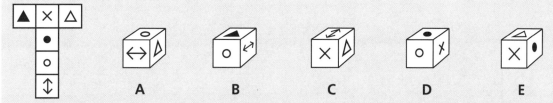

The correct answer is **C**. This has already been marked in Example i in Section 6 of Test Paper 1 of your answer sheet on page 172.

Example ii

Look at the two shapes on the left below. Find the connection between them and apply it to the third shape.

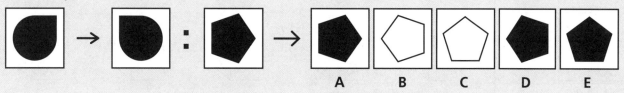

The correct answer is **D**. Mark the answer D in Example ii in Section 6 of Test Paper 1 of your answer sheet on page 172.

In questions 1–7, find which cube could be made from the given net.

1

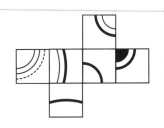

A   B   C   D   E

2

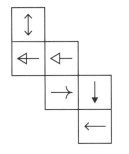

A   B   C   D   E

3

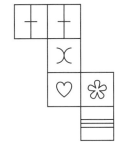

A   B   C   D   E

4

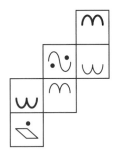

A   B   C   D   E

5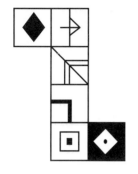

A   B   C   D   E

6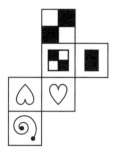

A   B   C   D   E

7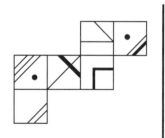

A   B   C   D   E

CONTINUE WORKING

In questions 8–13, you are given two figures with an arrow between them. On the next row, there is a new figure with an arrow pointing to five more figures. Decide which one of these five figures goes with the new figure to make a pair like the two above.

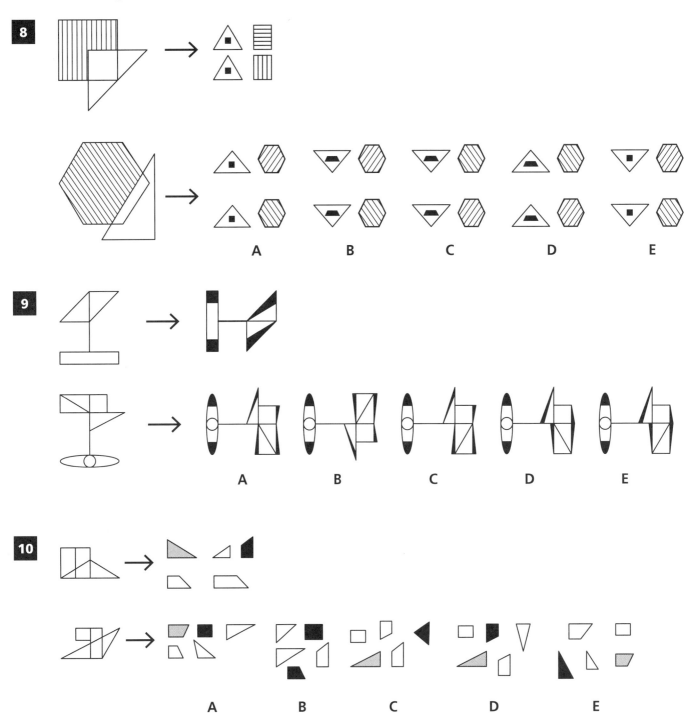

11

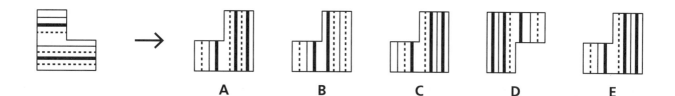

A   B   C   D   E

12

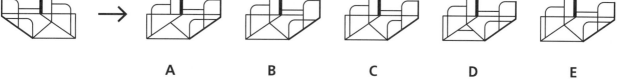

A   B   C   D   E

13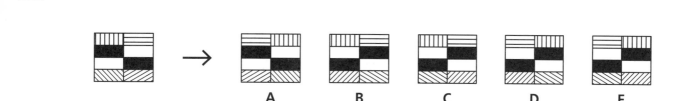

A   B   C   D   E

END OF PAPER

Collins

Test Paper 2

Instructions:

1. Ensure you have pencils and an eraser with you.

2. Make sure you are able to see a clock or watch.

3. Write your name on the answer sheet.

4. Do not start until you are told to do so by an adult.

5. Mark your answers on the answer sheet only.

6. All workings must be completed on a separate piece of paper.

7. You should not use a calculator, dictionary or thesaurus at any point in this paper.

8. Move through the sections as quickly as possible and with care.

9. Follow any instructions on each page.

10. You should mark your answers with a horizontal strike, as shown on the answer sheet.

11. If you want to change your answer, ensure that you rub out your first answer and that your second answer is clearly more visible.

12. You can go back and review any questions that are within the section you are working on only.

SECTION 1: PROBLEM SOLVING

 INSTRUCTIONS

 YOU HAVE 6 MINUTES TO COMPLETE THE FOLLOWING SECTION.

YOU HAVE 10 QUESTIONS TO COMPLETE WITHIN THE TIME GIVEN.

Select an answer to each question from the 10 different possible answers in the table below.

A 4.2 kg	B 18.8 kg	C 7.5 kg	D 4,500 g	E 8.4 kg
F 16.8 kg	G 10.6 kg	H 5,000 g	I 6.3 kg	J 500 g

Example i

My pet rabbit has a mass of 2,100 grams. My cat weighs twice as much.

My neighbour's dog has a mass that is four times greater than my cat.

What is the mass of my neighbour's dog?

The correct answer is **F**. This has already been marked in Example i in Section 1 of Test Paper 2 of your answer sheet on page 173.

Example ii

I buy a bag of rice with a mass of 10 kg. The next day, I use 25% of the bag to make some meals.

The following day, I use one-third of what is left in the bag.

How much rice is now left in the bag?

The correct answer is **H**. Mark the answer H in Example ii in Section 1 of Test Paper 2 of your answer sheet on page 173.

Test Paper 2

Several questions will follow for you to answer. Select an answer to each question from the 10 different possible answers in the table below. You may use an answer for more than one question.

A 10:57 am	B £14	C 2,500	D 50	E 250
F £14.50	G 10:56 am	H 500	I £13.50	J 45

1 Steve is decorating his bathroom. That morning, he went to a shop and spent £40.50 on three identical tins of paint.

How much was one tin of paint in the shop?

2 Steve then went on to another shop and bought a footstool at £9.38 and two brushes at £2.06 each.

How much did he spend in total at that shop?

3 Steve's journey to the shops and back covered 45 miles. It cost him 14p per mile in fuel, plus he spent £5.70 on a sandwich and £2.50 on a coffee during the journey.

What was the total cost of his journey?

4 Steve left that morning for the shops at 8:22 am. He spent 1 hour and 34 minutes driving, 18 minutes stopping for a sandwich and a coffee, 24 minutes in the first shop and 19 minutes in the second shop.

At what time did he return home?

5 Steve is going to tile the area above his sink. It has a width of 0.25 m and a height of 1 m.

How large is the area he needs to tile in cm²?

6 Steve has already bought tiles that measure 5 cm × 1 cm for the area.

How many tiles will he need to use?

7 During his lunch break, Steve calls a friend on his mobile phone. His phone company charges him 12p for the first 5 minutes of the call and 3p per minute thereafter.

If the call costs him £1.47 in total, how many minutes did the call last?

8 Steve uses a cloth which is a perfect rectangle shape. It has a length of 50 cm and a length-to-width ratio of 10 : 1

What is the area of the cloth in cm^2?

9 Steve takes 2 hours and 16 minutes to finish the tiling. He takes a quarter of that time to clean the floor. It takes him 11 minutes longer to refit the bathroom light than it did to clean the floor.

How many minutes did he spend refitting the bathroom light?

10 Steve still has a few jobs to finish the next day. He decides to have a lie-in and ends up starting work 1 hour and 17 minutes after waking up.

If he starts work at 12:14 pm, at what time did he wake up?

Test Paper 2

SECTION 2: CLOZE

| | INSTRUCTIONS | |

 YOU HAVE 8 MINUTES TO COMPLETE THE FOLLOWING SECTION.

YOU HAVE 20 QUESTIONS TO COMPLETE WITHIN THE TIME GIVEN.

Example i

Read the sentence below and select the most appropriate word from the table to complete it.

A	B	C	D	E
interesting	cunning	intellectual	promising	metallic

The **Question 1** fox showed no mercy to the little mouse.

The correct answer is **B**. This has already been marked in Example i in Section 2 of Test Paper 2 of your answer sheet on page 173.

Example ii

Read the sentence below and select the most appropriate word from the table to complete it.

A	B	C	D	E
adorned	improved	grown	flourished	destroyed

A late frost has completely **Question 2** Mum's flowers.

The correct answer is **E**. Mark the answer E in Example ii in Section 2 of Test Paper 2 of your answer sheet on page 173.

Read the passage below and select the most appropriate word from the table to fill each space. Mark the letter of the correct word on your answer sheet.

A	B	C	D	E
toll	contrast	wives	lavish	indulgence

F	G	H	I	J
eventually	boring	monarchs	perhaps	fun

King Henry VIII

Henry VIII, King of England and Ireland from 1509 until 1547, is perhaps one of the most famous **Question 1** in English history.

The young King Henry was **Question 2** , lively, clever and handsome, in **Question 3** to his **Question 4** father. He was over six feet tall and loved spending money.

Henry's hobbies were jousting, hunting, composing music and throwing **Question 5** parties. But as he grew older, all that **Question 6** took its **Question 7** on his physical health. Henry became very overweight and **Question 8** struggled to walk.

Henry is **Question 9** best known for having six **Question 10**!

CONTINUE WORKING

Test Paper 2

Read the passage below and select the most appropriate word from the table to fill each space. Mark the letter of the correct word on your answer sheet.

A	B	C	D	E
challenge	expedition	known	border	referred

F	G	H	I	J
perilous	summit	extreme	rapidity	peak

Mount Everest

Mount Everest lies on the **Question 11** of Nepal and Tibet. At 8,849 metres, it is the highest **Question 12** in the world.

In January, temperatures on the **Question 13** can drop as low as –60 degrees Celsius.

Climbers have been drawn to the **Question 14** of summiting Everest for many years.

The first successful summit was achieved in 1953 by a British **Question 15** when Edmund Hillary and Sherpa Tenzing became the first men **Question 16** to have reached the top.

Anything above 7,600 metres is **Question 17** to as the 'death zone'; at this altitude, the breathing and pulse rates of climbers increase significantly in **Question 18**, both symptoms of oxygen deprivation in the body tissues. This lack of oxygen can result in poor decision-making, which is **Question 19** in such **Question 20** conditions.

SECTION 3: NON-VERBAL ABILITY

 YOU HAVE 9 MINUTES TO COMPLETE THE FOLLOWING SECTION.

YOU HAVE 15 QUESTIONS TO COMPLETE WITHIN THE TIME GIVEN.

Example i

The figures on the left each have a code. Work out how the codes go with these figures.

Find the correct code on the right that matches the fifth figure.

BCG   ADG   AEF   BDF | ?   AEG BCF BDG ADF BEG

                                    A   **B**   **C**   **D**   **E**

The first letter indicates whether the arrow is pointing up or down: A – up; B – down. The second letter is for the style of the arrowhead: C – triangular head; D – diamond head; E – round head. The third letter codes for whether the arrow is pointing left or right: F – right; G – left. The fifth shape is pointing down (B), has a round arrowhead (E) and is pointing to the left (G). The answer is BEG.

The correct answer is therefore **E**. This has already been marked in Example i in Section 3 of Test Paper 2 of your answer sheet on page 173.

Examples ii and iii

Look at figures A and B. They are then rotated. Match the two rotations labelled ii and iii to each of the original figures A and B.

                A   **B**   **ii**   **iii**

Example ii

The correct answer is **B**. Mark the answer B in Example ii in Section 3 of Test Paper 2 of your answer sheet on page 173.

Example iii

The correct answer is **A**. Mark the answer A in Example iii in Section 3 of Test Paper 2 of your answer sheet on page 173.

Test Paper 2

In questions 1–8, the figures on the left each have a code. Work out how the codes go with these figures. Then look at the figure on the right of the vertical line and find its code from the five options given.

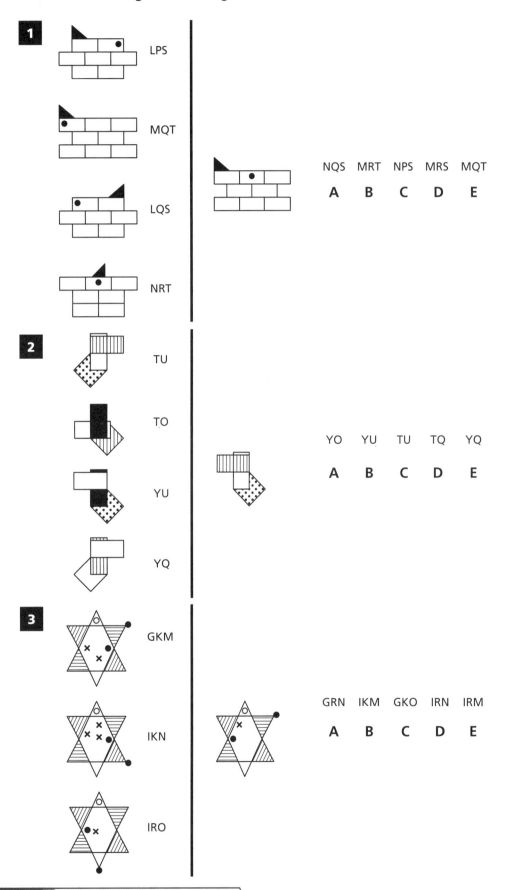

1

LPS

MQT

LQS

NRT

NQS   MRT   NPS   MRS   MQT

A   B   C   D   E

2

TU

TO

YU

YQ

YO   YU   TU   TQ   YQ

A   B   C   D   E

3

GKM

IKN

IRO

GRN   IKM   GKO   IRN   IRM

A   B   C   D   E

4

 FJW

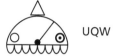 UQW

 FQZ

 UKX

FKW UQZ FJX UKW FKX

A   B   C   D   E

5

 ORN

 OSM

PTM

PSN OTM PRN PSM OTN

A   B   C   D   E

6

 DZA

 PZB

 VWB

VWB DWB DZA PWB PZA

A   B   C   D   E

CONTINUE WORKING ⇨

7

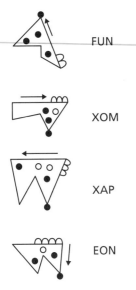

FUN

XOM

XAP

EON

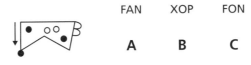

FAN	XOP	FON	EAM	FUM
A	B	C	D	E

8

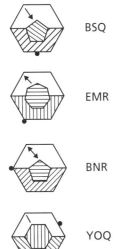

BSQ

EMR

BNR

YOQ

ENQ	BSQ	YMR	BOQ	ESR
A	B	C	D	E

For questions 9–15, match figures 9–15 to their rotations A–G.

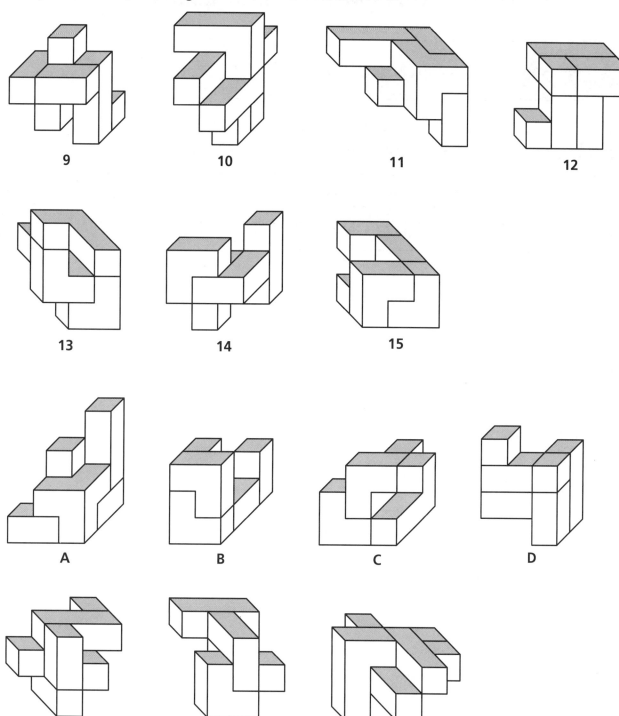

9

10

11

12

13

14

15

A

B

C

D

E

F

G

Test Paper 2

SECTION 4: GRAMMAR AND SPELLING

 INSTRUCTIONS

 YOU HAVE 4 MINUTES TO COMPLETE THE FOLLOWING SECTION.

YOU HAVE 10 QUESTIONS TO COMPLETE WITHIN THE TIME GIVEN.

Example i

What type of word is 'incredible'?

A	B	C	D	E
adverb	adjective	verb	noun	conjunction

The correct answer is **B**. This has already been marked in Example i in Section 4 of Test Paper 2 of your answer sheet on page 174.

Example ii

Select the word that has been misspelt.

A	B	C	D	E
rearrange	flimsy	enviroment	lonely	reliable

The correct answer is **C**. Mark the answer C in Example ii in Section 4 of Test Paper 2 of your answer sheet on page 174.

1 Select the homophone for the word 'brake'.

A	B	C	D	E
break	broke	broken	brick	bracken

2 Select the correct prefix to make the opposite meaning of the word 'plausible'.

A	B	C	D	E
dis	mis	in	im	un

3 Select the word that has been misspelt.

A	B	C	D	E
forage	marraige	calamity	silhouette	disappearance

4 What type of word is 'indigenous'?

A	B	C	D	E
adverb	noun	adjective	verb	determiner

5 Select the word that can be used as an adverb.

A	B	C	D	E
admit	breathless	exhausting	lovely	fast

6 Select the word that has been misspelt.

A	B	C	D	E
psychologically	aquisition	granite	belligerent	ordinarily

7 Complete this word by inserting the missing letters.

a c _ _ s t i c

8 Complete this word by inserting the missing letters.

c o _ r a g _ _ _ s

9 Complete this word by inserting the missing letters.

d e f _ n _ t _ l y

10 Complete this word by inserting the missing letters.

c o n _ _ _ o u s n e s s

Test Paper 2

SECTION 5: ANTONYMS

 INSTRUCTIONS

 YOU HAVE 7 MINUTES TO COMPLETE THE FOLLOWING SECTION.

YOU HAVE 15 QUESTIONS TO COMPLETE WITHIN THE TIME GIVEN.

Example i

Select the word that is most opposite in meaning to the following word:

courageous

A	B	C	D	E
brave	fierce	kind	shy	cowardly

The correct answer is **E**. This has already been marked in Example i in Section 5 of Test Paper 2 of your answer sheet on page 174.

Example ii

Select the word that is most opposite in meaning to the following word:

tie

A	B	C	D	E
wrap	undo	stitch	knit	lace

The correct answer is **B**. Mark the answer B in Example ii in Section 5 of Test Paper 2 of your answer sheet on page 174.

Select the word that is most opposite in meaning to the given word.

1 lavish

A	B	C	D	E
opulent	varied	stingy	generous	wondrous

2 summit

A	B	C	D	E
top	peak	edge	base	side

3 powerful

A	B	C	D	E
impotent	thin	potent	great	giant

4 attract

A	B	C	D	E
distract	disapprove	distort	fancy	repel

5 follow

A	B	C	D	E
after	precede	pursue	next	queue

6 restore

A	B	C	D	E
hoard	gather	store	relapse	reason

7 severe

A	B	C	D	E
strict	lenient	cross	gentle	cut

CONTINUE WORKING

8 respect

A	B	C	D	E
fury	disbelief	disappointment	loyalty	contempt

9 disclose

A	B	C	D	E
hide	discover	produce	open	shut

10 lower

A	B	C	D	E
lessen	high	diminish	illuminate	elevate

11 plain

A	B	C	D	E
submarine	land	ornate	desert	complain

12 vigorous

A	B	C	D	E
strong	mighty	unstable	feeble	thin

13 brittle

A	B	C	D	E
vicious	tough	fragile	transparent	rough

14 trivial

A	B	C	D	E
nonsense	three-sided	overrated	important	forgettable

15 reservation

A	B	C	D	E
cancellation	doubt	certainty	booking	qualm

SECTION 6: NUMERACY

 INSTRUCTIONS

 YOU HAVE 9 MINUTES TO COMPLETE THE FOLLOWING SECTION.

YOU HAVE 18 QUESTIONS TO COMPLETE WITHIN THE TIME GIVEN.

Example i

Calculate 42 + 23

A	B	C	D	E
62	61	64	65	66

The correct answer is **D**. This has already been marked in Example i in Section 6 of Test Paper 2 of your answer sheet on page 174.

Example ii

Chloe leaves school at 3:42 pm and arrives home 39 minutes later.

At what time does she arrive home?

A	B	C	D	E
4:23 pm	4:21 pm	4:31 pm	4:11 pm	4:12 pm

The correct answer is **B**. Mark the answer B in Example ii in Section 6 of Test Paper 2 of your answer sheet on page 174.

Test Paper 2

1 What is the correct expression for the perimeter of this square?

$4y + 3$

A	B	C	D	E
$8y + 6$	$16y + 9$	$16y + 12$	$8y + 12$	$12y + 12$

2 In the square in question 1, $y = 3$. The units are centimetres.

What is the area of the square?

A	B	C	D	E
$250\,cm^2$	$121\,cm^2$	$144\,cm^2$	$300\,cm^2$	$225\,cm^2$

3 A circle has a diameter of 25 cm.

What is its radius?

A	B	C	D	E
50 cm	12 cm	25 cm	54 cm	12.5 cm

4 Calculate $\frac{4}{5} + \frac{3}{20}$

A	B	C	D	E
$\frac{19}{20}$	$\frac{2}{3}$	$\frac{9}{10}$	$\frac{17}{20}$	$\frac{5}{6}$

5 Calculate $\frac{2}{3} \times \frac{3}{4}$

A	B	C	D	E
$\frac{1}{2}$	$\frac{1}{4}$	$\frac{1}{3}$	$\frac{3}{5}$	$\frac{5}{6}$

6 Calculate $\frac{3}{5} - \frac{1}{6}$

A	B	C	D	E
$\frac{2}{15}$	$\frac{1}{4}$	$\frac{4}{15}$	$\frac{13}{30}$	$\frac{2}{7}$

7 I roll two fair, six-sided dice. What is the probability that they both land on 6?

A	B	C	D	E
$\frac{1}{12}$	$\frac{1}{6}$	$\frac{1}{36}$	$\frac{2}{15}$	$\frac{1}{3}$

8 What is the size of the smallest angle between the two hands of a clock at half-past three?

A	B	C	D	E
80°	90°	75°	65°	110°

9 How many of these shapes have four straight sides of equal length?

parallelogram   square   trapezium   kite   rhombus

A	B	C	D	E
4	3	2	1	0

10 If a cup holds 300 ml, how many cups would it take to fill a 9-litre bottle?

A	B	C	D	E
300	33	30	3	27

11 Sophia is planning for her flight at the weekend. It departs at 9:45 am. She wants to be at the airport 2 hours and 15 minutes before it leaves. She is getting a taxi from her house to the airport, which is a 36-minute journey.

At what time should she book the taxi for?

A	B	C	D	E
6:54 am	6:48 am	6:56 am	6:44 am	7:04 am

12 A group of children are asked which sports they play in the summer term and the results are shown in the Venn diagram.

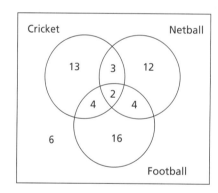

What percentage of those asked didn't play any of the sports?

A	B	C	D	E
5%	10%	15%	20%	25%

13 Using the Venn diagram in question 12, what fraction of those asked played football?

A	B	C	D	E
$\frac{4}{15}$	$\frac{1}{4}$	$\frac{1}{3}$	$\frac{13}{30}$	$\frac{2}{5}$

CONTINUE WORKING

14 What is six to the power of three plus three cubed?

A	B	C	D	E
27	243	233	240	237

15 What is the next number in this sequence?

17, 24, 41, 65, ...

A	B	C	D	E
106	89	90	88	92

16 What is the total surface area of this triangular prism?

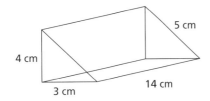

A	B	C	D	E
240 cm²	150 cm²	160 cm²	170 cm²	180 cm²

17 A number machine takes an input, quadruples it, then adds 29 to get an output.

What is the input when the output is 97?

A	B	C	D	E
17	15	16	18	19

18 A car park charges £2.50 for every two hours from 8 am to 8 pm and 80p for every hour parked outside of those hours.

If I park my car at 12 noon and collect it ten hours later, what will I be charged?

A	B	C	D	E
£12	£21.60	£21.80	£11.60	£11.80

END OF PAPER

Collins

Test Paper 3

Instructions:

1. Ensure you have pencils and an eraser with you.
2. Make sure you are able to see a clock or watch.
3. Write your name on the answer sheet.
4. Do not start until you are told to do so by an adult.
5. Mark your answers on the answer sheet only.
6. All workings must be completed on a separate piece of paper.
7. You should not use a calculator, dictionary or thesaurus at any point in this paper.
8. Move through the sections as quickly as possible and with care.
9. Follow any instructions on each page.
10. You should mark your answers with a horizontal strike, as shown on the answer sheet.
11. If you want to change your answer, ensure that you rub out your first answer and that your second answer is clearly more visible.
12. You can go back and review any questions that are within the section you are working on only.

SECTION 1: COMPREHENSION

 INSTRUCTIONS

 YOU HAVE 12 MINUTES TO COMPLETE THE FOLLOWING SECTION.

YOU HAVE 14 QUESTIONS TO COMPLETE WITHIN THE TIME GIVEN.

We didn't realise what had happened until we heard a helicopter passing over the roof of our house.

It was an air ambulance and it landed next to the main road. One of our neighbours then told us that there had been a car crash near the corner shop and somebody was seriously injured.

Example i

What landed next to the main road?

A   A plane

B   A hot-air balloon

C   A glider

D   A helicopter

The correct answer is **D**. This has already been marked in Example i in Section 1 of Test Paper 3 of your answer sheet on page 175.

Example ii

Who said there had been a car accident?

A   A neighbour

B   A police officer

C   A paramedic

D   A shopkeeper

The correct answer is **A**. Mark the answer A in Example ii in Section 1 of Test Paper 3 of your answer sheet on page 175.

Read the passage below and then answer the questions that follow.

Three Men in a Boat

by Jerome K Jerome

> *In the passage, three friends have decided to travel along the River Thames and are camping near the village of Sonning. They have brought their dog, Montmorency.*

1 We roamed about sweet Sonning for an hour or so, and then, it being too late to push on past Reading, we decided to go back to one of the Shiplake islands, and put up there for the night. It was still early when we got settled, and George said that, as we had plenty of time, it would be a splendid opportunity to try a good, slap-up supper. He said he would show us what could be done

5 up the river in the way of cooking, and suggested that, with the vegetables and the remains of the cold beef and general odds and ends, we should make an Irish stew.

It seemed a fascinating idea. George gathered wood and made a fire, and Harris and I started to peel the potatoes. I should never have thought that peeling potatoes was such an undertaking. The job turned out to be the biggest thing of its kind that I had ever been in. We

10 began cheerfully, one might almost say skittishly, but our light-heartedness was gone by the time the first potato was finished. The more we peeled, the more peel there seemed to be left on; by the time we had got all the peel off and all the eyes out, there was no potato left – at least none worth speaking of. George came and had a look at it – it was about the size of a pea-nut. He said: "Oh, that won't do! You're wasting them. You must scrape them."

15 So we scraped them, and that was harder work than peeling. They are such an extraordinary shape, potatoes – all bumps and warts and hollows. We worked steadily for five-and-twenty minutes, and did four potatoes. Then we struck. We said we should require the rest of the evening for scraping ourselves.

I never saw such a thing as potato-scraping for making a fellow in a mess. It seemed difficult to

20 believe that the potato-scrapings in which Harris and I stood, half smothered, could have come off four potatoes. It shows you what can be done with economy and care.

George said it was absurd to have only four potatoes in an Irish stew, so we washed half-a-dozen or so more, and put them in without peeling. We also put in a cabbage and about half a peck of peas. George stirred it all up, and then he said that there seemed to be a lot of room to spare, so

25 we overhauled both the hampers, and picked out all the odds and ends and the remnants, and added them to the stew. […] Then George found half a tin of potted salmon, and he emptied that into the pot.

CONTINUE WORKING

He said that was the advantage of Irish stew: you got rid of such a lot of things. I fished out a couple of eggs that had got cracked, and put those in. George said they would thicken the gravy.

30 I forget the other ingredients, but I know nothing was wasted; and I remember that, towards the end, Montmorency, who had evinced great interest in the proceedings throughout, strolled away with an earnest and thoughtful air, reappearing, a few minutes afterwards, with a dead water-rat in his mouth, which he evidently wished to present as his contribution to the dinner; whether in a sarcastic spirit, or with a genuine desire to assist, I cannot say.

35 We had a discussion as to whether the rat should go in or not. Harris said that he thought it would be all right, mixed up with the other things, and that every little helped; but George stood up for precedent. He said he had never heard of water-rats in Irish stew, and he would rather be on the safe side, and not try experiments.

Harris said:

40 "If you never try a new thing, how can you tell what it's like? It's men such as you that hamper the world's progress."

1 **What does 'put up' (line 2) mean in the context of this story?**

A Tolerate

B Camp

C Become quiet

D Construct

2 **How did Harris and the narrator deal with the potatoes initially?**

A Exuberantly peeling, with enthusiasm, until only a small amount of one potato was left.

B Exuberantly peeling, with enthusiasm, until only a small amount of four potatoes was left.

C They did not enjoy peeling the first potato and were very slapdash in how they peeled it.

D Exuberantly scraping, with enthusiasm, until only a small amount of one potato was left.

3 **Why does the narrator say 'It shows you what can be done with economy and care' (line 21)?**

A He is reiterating that scraping potatoes is messier than peeling.

B He is showing that scraping potatoes is much tidier than peeling.

C The men have been careful as they scraped the potatoes.

D He is being sarcastic.

4 How did the men feel after having scraped four potatoes?

A Exhausted   **B** Incredulous   **C** Jovial   **D** Oppressed

5 How many potatoes were eventually put into the stew?

A Ten   **B** Six   **C** Four   **D** Around 11

6 What else was put into the stew?

i   Cabbage   ii   Peas

iii Eggs   iv   Rat

v   Salmon

A All of the above

B i, ii and iii

C All except ii and iv

D We do not know the full list of ingredients.

7 What is suggested about the travellers' personalities?

A They are enthusiastic but haphazard.

B They enjoy teasing each other.

C They are generally confused.

D They are inventive and resourceful.

8 Which of the characters seems to be the most dominant in the extract?

A Montmorency   **B** The narrator   **C** George   **D** Harris

9 How does the writer create a specific tone in the passage?

A The narrator is trying to make the passage seem as absurd in tone as possible.

B He makes it humorous and lighthearted, as if the narrator does not know how funny he is.

C Describing the travellers' cooking makes the passage seem horrific and unpleasant.

D The story is intended as a moral to encourage readers to co-operate with team members.

CONTINUE WORKING

10 **Why does the writer mention the travellers' dog's reaction to the stew being cooked?**

   A It creates humour as it seems as though the dog mimics the men's culinary endeavours.

   B It shows that the men care about their dog enormously.

   C It makes the men's surroundings seem dirty and extremely unpleasant to be in.

   D It creates contrast with the men's pleasant campsite.

11 **What does Harris mean in lines 40–41 of the extract?**

   A Being afraid of new things is counterproductive.

   B Standing up for yourself generally slows down processes in the world.

   C People who are afraid of experimentation hinder the progress of humankind.

   D People who are negative hold others back.

12 **What is a 'slap-up supper' (line 4)?**

   A A meal with only the most expensive, luxurious ingredients

   B A special, particularly enjoyable, meal

   C Something to celebrate a specific occasion

   D A meal that can be prepared quickly and without much fuss

13 **Which of the following words is closest in meaning to 'remnants' (line 25)?**

   A Provisions

   B Ingredients

   C Delicacies

   D Leftover pieces

14 **Which of the following words is closest in meaning to 'evinced' (line 31)?**

   A Accepted

   B Demonstrated

   C Sniffed

   D Moved delicately

SECTION 2: ODD ONE OUT

 INSTRUCTIONS

 YOU HAVE 7 MINUTES TO COMPLETE THE FOLLOWING SECTION.

YOU HAVE 15 QUESTIONS TO COMPLETE WITHIN THE TIME GIVEN.

Example i

Four of these words are related in some way. Select the word that does not go with the other four.

A	B	C	D	E
expand	increase	contract	enlarge	spread

The correct answer is **C**. This has already been marked in Example i in Section 2 of Test Paper 3 of your answer sheet on page 175.

Example ii

Four of these words are related in some way. Select the word that does not go with the other four.

A	B	C	D	E
sweet	sour	sharp	bitter	acidic

The correct answer is **A**. Mark the answer A in Example ii in Section 2 of Test Paper 3 of your answer sheet on page 175.

Test Paper 3

In each question, four of the words are related in some way. Select the word that does not go with the other four.

1

A	B	C	D	E
malodour	stench	fragrant	fetidity	foul

2

A	B	C	D	E
discord	conflict	jar	harmony	grate

3

A	B	C	D	E
luminous	radiant	illuminated	fluorescent	sombre

4

A	B	C	D	E
pallid	florid	ruddy	vivid	high-coloured

5

A	B	C	D	E
abruptly	unawares	suddenly	expectantly	instantaneously

6

A	B	C	D	E
French	Welsh	Italy	Spanish	Russian

7

A	B	C	D	E
strap	soul	lace	heel	toe

8

A	B	C	D	E
dense	solid	ethereal	firm	concrete

9

A	B	C	D	E
preposition	prefix	pronoun	adjective	noun

10

A	B	C	D	E
agitate	judder	jerk	jolt	reciprocate

11

A	B	C	D	E
belief	credit	conviction	denial	credence

12

A	B	C	D	E
inane	wise	sage	intelligent	sharp

13

A	B	C	D	E
exertion	effort	repose	strain	toil

14

A	B	C	D	E
counsel	speech	advice	advocate	commend

15

A	B	C	D	E
cunning	sly	artful	artless	crafty

SECTION 3: NUMERACY

 INSTRUCTIONS

 YOU HAVE 8 MINUTES TO COMPLETE THE FOLLOWING SECTION.

YOU HAVE 18 QUESTIONS TO COMPLETE WITHIN THE TIME GIVEN.

The questions within this section are not multiple choice. Write the answer to each question on the answer sheet by selecting the correct digits from the columns provided.

Example i

Calculate   34 + 51

The correct answer is **85**. This has already been marked in Example i in Section 3 of Test Paper 3 of your answer sheet on page 175.

Example ii

Calculate   75 ÷ 15

The correct answer is **5**. Mark the answer 05 in Example ii in Section 3 of Test Paper 3 of your answer sheet on page 175. Note that a single-digit answer should be marked with a 0 in the left-hand column.

Calculate the following.

1 Work out the answer to the following:

14 + 23 + 15

2 Add twelve to one-fifth of 75.

What is the answer?

3 Find the number that completes the sequence in place of the ?

18, 29, 39, 48, 56, ?

4 What is one hundred and eight minus thirty-nine?

5 How many factors of 24 have two digits?

6 Find the sum of the first five square numbers.

Read this information for questions 7–9.

Heather plays for her local cricket team. She plays six innings and ends up with a mean score of 48.

7 If Heather scored 24, 0, 99, 0 and 88 in her first five innings, what did she score in her final innings?

8 What was Heather's mode score after six innings?

9 What was the range in Heather's scores after six innings?

CONTINUE WORKING

10 I am twice as old as my brother. My grandmother is three times older than me. If we have 99 years between us, how old am I?

11 How many hours are there in a fourteenth of a week?

12 What is five cubed minus nine squared?

13 Round 55 to the nearest 10 and add 22 rounded to the nearest 10. What is the answer?

14 What are the total lines of symmetry on these letters?

A   C   J   F   Q   T

15 Find the number that completes the sequence in place of the ?

5, 4, 9, 13, 22, ?

16 Calculate: $-5 + 24 - 6$

17 How many minutes are there between 8:49 am and 9:24 am?

18 What is the lowest common multiple of 12 and 15?

SECTION 4: NON-VERBAL ABILITY

 INSTRUCTIONS

 YOU HAVE 9 MINUTES TO COMPLETE THE FOLLOWING SECTION.

YOU HAVE 14 QUESTIONS TO COMPLETE WITHIN THE TIME GIVEN.

Example i

Select how the shape on the left would appear when reflected in the dashed line.

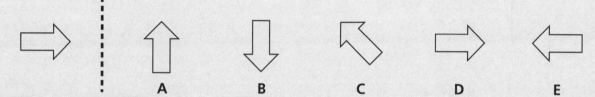

The correct answer is **E**. This has already been marked in Example i in Section 4 of Test Paper 3 on your answer sheet on page 176.

Example ii

The three figures on the left are similar in some way. Work out how they are similar and select the figure on the right that goes with them.

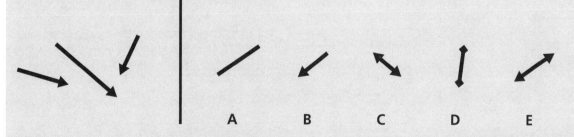

The correct answer is **B**. Mark the answer B in Example ii in Section 4 of Test Paper 3 on your answer sheet on page 176.

In questions 1–7, look at the figure on the left-hand side. Imagine it has been reflected in the vertical mirror line.

Select the correct answer option to show the reflection for each question.

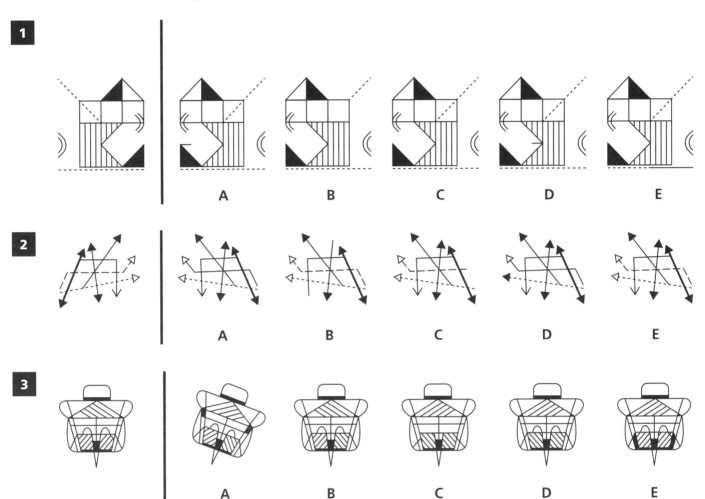

1

     A   B   C   D   E

2

     A   B   C   D   E

3

     A   B   C   D   E

4

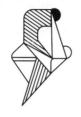    

A   B   C   D   E

5

A   B   C   D   E

6

A   B   C   D   E

7

     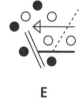

A   B   C   D   E

CONTINUE WORKING ➡

In questions 8–14, work out what makes the two figures on the left similar to each other.

Then find the figure on the right that is most like the two figures on the left.

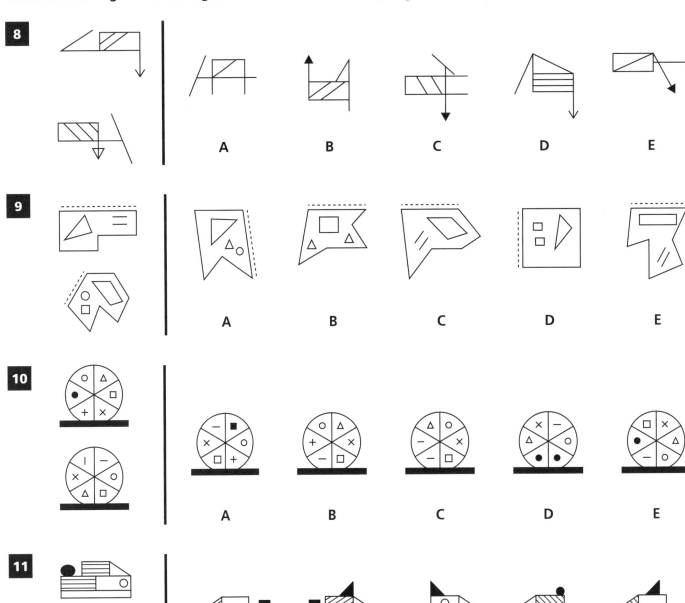

12

A B C D E

13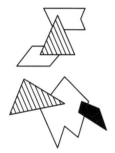

A B C D E

14

A B C D E

SECTION 5: WORD DEFINITIONS

 INSTRUCTIONS

 YOU HAVE 7 MINUTES TO COMPLETE THE FOLLOWING SECTION.

YOU HAVE 15 QUESTIONS TO COMPLETE WITHIN THE TIME GIVEN.

Example i

The teacher had a frank discussion with Kyle's parents.

What does the word 'frank' mean?

A	B	C	D	E
sincere	troubled	interesting	informative	brief

The correct answer is **A**. This has already been marked in Example i in Section 5 of Test Paper 3 of your answer sheet on page 176.

Example ii

The vendor agreed to sign the house over punctually at 3 pm.

What does the word 'vendor' mean?

A	B	C	D	E
purchaser	buyer	seller	agent	renter

The correct answer is **C**. Mark the answer C in Example ii in Section 5 of Test Paper 3 of your answer sheet on page 176.

Read each sentence and select the most appropriate word to answer each question.

Dolefully, Joel approached the little cottage where his infamous late grandfather had once lived.

1   What does the word 'dolefully' mean?

A	B	C	D	E
joyfully	mournfully	desperately	calmly	expectantly

2   What does the word 'infamous' mean?

A	B	C	D	E
famous	popular	celebrity	dedicated	notorious

An exquisite bird landed on the lawn as the arborist was finishing her work.

3   What does the word 'exquisite' mean?

A	B	C	D	E
enormous	exceptional	grotesque	colourful	beautiful

4   What does the word 'arborist' mean?

A	B	C	D	E
lumberjack	gardener	handyman	workman	builder

The knight came on stage-right, brandishing an authentic sword which could have done some serious damage in the wrong hands.

5   What does the word 'brandishing' mean?

A	B	C	D	E
holding	hiding	dragging	waving	tapping

6   What does the word 'authentic' mean?

A	B	C	D	E
original	artificial	steel	synthetic	genuine

Martha made an oblique reference to the heated discussion between her and Dev yesterday.

7   What does the word 'oblique' mean?

A	B	C	D	E
sinister	unclear	obvious	doubtful	courageous

CONTINUE WORKING

Test Paper 3

Aidan's blatant lie only served to cause irreparable harm to his relationship with Keir.

8   What does the word 'blatant' mean?

A	B	C	D	E
disgraceful	obvious	unpleasant	unfortunate	cunning

9   What does the word 'irreparable' mean?

A	B	C	D	E
irrevocable	irregular	inappropriate	irresponsible	irreplaceable

Our recent trip to the Lake District exceeded all our expectations and the general consensus is that we shall return in the autumn.

10   What does the word 'exceeded' mean?

A	B	C	D	E
ruined	excited	superseded	preceded	surpassed

11   What does the word 'consensus' mean?

A	B	C	D	E
consideration	admission	revelation	discussion	concurrence

Harry's teacher reproached him when he once again forgot the obligatory 'no talking in tests' rule.

12   What does the word 'reproached' mean?

A	B	C	D	E
encouraged	reminded	teased	chastised	detained

13   What does the word 'obligatory' mean?

A	B	C	D	E
advisable	recommended	compulsory	legal	dutiful

Felix is quite negligent in looking after the family's latest acquisition: a rather inert stick insect.

14   What does the word 'negligent' mean?

A	B	C	D	E
enthusiastic	careless	reliable	capable	careful

15   What does the word 'inert' mean?

A	B	C	D	E
motionless	skinny	weird	spritely	boring

SECTION 6: PROBLEM SOLVING

 INSTRUCTIONS

 YOU HAVE 6 MINUTES TO COMPLETE THE FOLLOWING SECTION.

YOU HAVE 13 QUESTIONS TO COMPLETE WITHIN THE TIME GIVEN.

Example i

I buy one adult ticket and two child tickets for a tram journey. An adult ticket costs £4.30 and a child ticket costs £2.40

How much change do I receive from £10?

A	B	C	D	E
£1.90	£1.30	£3.30	70p	90p

The correct answer is **E**. This has already been marked in Example i in Section 6 of Test Paper 3 of your answer sheet on page 176.

Example ii

There are 30 children in a class. 60% of the children in the class are girls.

How many boys are in the class?

A	B	C	D	E
6	18	8	12	10

The correct answer is **D**. Mark the answer D in Example ii in Section 6 of Test Paper 3 of your answer sheet on page 176.

Test Paper 3

1 Shona ate three-quarters of a pizza and her friend then ate half of what remained.

How much pizza is now left?

A	B	C	D	E
one-half	one-eighth	one-sixth	one-seventh	one-tenth

2 What percentage of this shape is shaded?

A	B	C	D	E
5%	12.5%	25%	20%	15%

3 What is the value of $x + y$ in this diagram?
The arrowed lines are parallel to each other.

A	B	C	D	E
126°	120°	125°	140°	136°

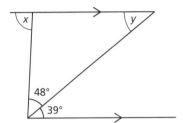

4 What is the perimeter of this parallelogram?

A	B	C	D	E
$32x + 15$	$32x + 8$	$16x + 16$	$16x + 8$	$32x + 16$

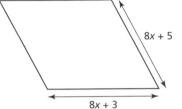

$8x + 5$

$8x + 3$

5 24 apples cost £8.40

How much would 7 apples cost?

A	B	C	D	E
£4.20	£2.30	£2.35	£2.45	£2.50

6 Paula went to the shop with a £20 note. She bought 3 magazines at £3.75 each, a sandwich for £2.18 and two packets of chewing gum at 80p each.

How much change did she receive?

A	B	C	D	E
£5.03	£4.83	£4.91	£5	£4.97

7 Calculate $44 + (6 \times 5) \div 2$

A	B	C	D	E
56	128	59	125	501

8 What is the size of the smaller angle between the two hands of a clock at 1:30?

A	B	C	D	E
120°	115°	105°	135°	125°

9   What number is 1.47 more than 8.92?

A	B	C	D	E
10.39	10.29	10.19	10.42	10.33

10   On the grid, plot a triangle at point A (–6, –2), B (–6, –5), C (–3, –2).

Now reflect the triangle in the *y*-axis.

What are the new coordinates of point C?

A	B	C	D	E
(3, 2)	(–3, –2)	(5, 3)	(4, –1)	(3, –2)

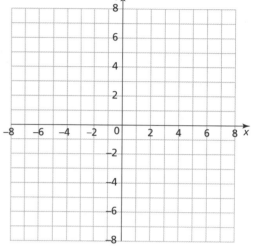

11   In five tests, Anni scored 74, 58, 82, 58 and 64. Add the range of her scores to her mode score.

What is the answer?

A	B	C	D	E
68	82	72	80	76

12   Asif leaves his house at 8:20 am. He drives at an average speed of 50 mph and arrives at his friend's house at 9:50 am.

What is the distance between Asif's house and his friend's house?

A	B	C	D	E
100 miles	70 miles	75 miles	80 miles	90 miles

13   At a café, Ben buys 3 cakes and 4 coffees at a total cost of £7.60. At the same café, his friend buys 2 cakes and 8 coffees at a total cost of £10.40

How much does one coffee cost in the café?

A	B	C	D	E
£1.10	£1.05	£1.15	£1	£1.20

END OF PAPER

Answers

Award 1 mark per correct answer unless otherwise stated.

Numerical Ability Activities

Pages 10–11

Challenge 1
a) 4   b) 3   c) 4   d) 2   e) 8   f) 2

Challenge 2
a) 9   b) 3   c) 3   d) 3   e) 3   f) 1

Challenge 3
a) 7.1   b) 7.21   c) 0.77   d) 3.87
e) 23.6

Challenge 4
a) 248.25   b) 395   c) 1,212.50
d) 302.524   e) 53.94218   f) 0.000414

Now Try This!
1.   C
    Multiplying by 0.01 means moving the decimal point two places to the left. Therefore 52,481.3952 becomes 524.813952
2.   a)   A
        Work out the decimal point movements overall. 28.4 = one to the right, 1.432 = one to the left, so no movement and answer remains the same at 40.6688
    b)   E
        284 = two to the right, 0.1432 = two to the left. So again the same answer of 40.6688

Pages 12–13

Challenge 1
a) 85   b) 313   c) 299   d) 4,468
e) 1,081   f) 18,365   g) 77   h) 2,656

Challenge 2
a) 228   b) 16.2   c) 6,293.50   d) 25
e) 9,984   f) 24   g) 1,840.80   h) 116.7

Challenge 3

23	×	7	=	161
725	+	346	=	1,071
77	÷	11	=	7
64	×	0.01	=	0.64
1.5	×	0.5	=	0.75
300	×	0.25	=	75
400	÷	5	=	80
10,000	×	0.0001	=	1
0.352	×	1,000	=	352
0.5	÷	2	=	0.25

Challenge 4
a)   182 marbles
    14 × 13 = 182
b)   £146
    217 – 25 – 46 = 146
c)   £7.70
    First 20 minutes at 25p per minute =
    20 × 0.25 = £5
    Next 18 minutes at 15p = 18 × 0.15 = £2.70
    £5 + £2.70 = £7.70

Now Try This!
1.   A
    3,229 – 682 = 2,547

2.   D
    Full price fares: 265 × £3.50 = £927.50
    Remainder of people = 483 – 265 = 218
    Half-price fare = $\frac{£3.50}{2}$ = £1.75
    £1.75 × 218 = £381.50
    Total spent = £927.50 + £381.50 = £1,309

Pages 14–15

Challenge 1

Fraction	Decimal	Percentage
$\frac{1}{2}$	0.5	50
$\frac{1}{4}$	0.25	25
$\frac{2}{5}$	0.4	40
$\frac{1}{5}$	0.2	20
$\frac{1}{10}$	0.1	10
$\frac{9}{20}$	0.45	45
$\frac{7}{25}$	0.28	28
$\frac{11}{50}$	0.22	22

Challenge 2
a) 0.12   b) $\frac{2}{5}$ c) 60%   d) 62.5%
e) $\frac{3}{20}$ f) $\frac{3}{5}$ g) 100%

Challenge 3
a) $\frac{2}{3}$
    $\frac{10}{15}$ simplified to $\frac{2}{3}$
b)   80%
    $\frac{4}{5}$ so $\frac{80}{100}$ = 80%

Challenge 4
a)   8 circles shaded
    20 circles so shade in 20 × 0.4 = 8
b)   3 circles shaded
    15 circles so shade in 15 × 0.2 = 3

Now Try This!
1.   D
    Work out $\frac{2}{5}$ of 6,500: $\frac{6,500}{5}$ = 1,300
    1,300 × 2 = 2,600
    2,600 × 0.35 = 910
2.   D
    We know that 33 marks = 55%
    So $\frac{33}{x}$ = $\frac{55}{100}$, $\frac{3,300}{x}$ = 55, x = 60
    Lou got 65% so 60 × 0.65 = 39. Lou got 6 more marks than Min.

Pages 16–17

Challenge 1
a) 4 : 1   b) 8 : 7
c) 3 : 1 ratio, add ratios to get 4. $\frac{24}{4}$ = 6, 6 × 3 = £18   d) 6 : 3 : 1

Challenge 2
a)   36
    The ratio is 6 : 1. Add the ratios to get 7.
    $\frac{42}{7}$ = 6, 6 × Edith's ratio of 6 = 36
b)   £40
    The ratio is 5 : 4. Add the ratios to get 9.
    $\frac{90}{9}$ = 10, 10 × Clara's ratio of 4 = £40
c)   42
    The ratio is 4 : 3. Add the ratios to get 7.
    $\frac{98}{7}$ = 14. 14 × girls' ratio of 3 = 42

Challenge 3

Boys	Girls	Ratio
15	20	3 : 4
12	18	2 : 3
8	10	4 : 5
6	15	2 : 5
28	16	7 : 4

Challenge 4
a)   12 : 3 : 1
b)   £150
    The ratio is 6 : 3 : 1. Add the ratios to get 10.
    $\frac{500}{10}$ = 50, 50 × Carole's ratio of 3 = £150
c)   £12
    The ratio is 12 : 6 : 1. Add the ratios to get 19.
    $\frac{228}{19}$ = 12, 12 × Wayne's ratio of 1 = £12
d)   14
    Ratio = 0.5 : 1 : 3. Add the ratios to get 4.5.
    $\frac{63}{4.5}$ = 14, 14 × Ranjeet's ratio of 1 = 14

Now Try This!
1.   C
    A quarter of 200 = $\frac{200}{4}$ = 50
    Of the 150 left, ratio is 2 : 1.
    Add the ratios to get 3.
    $\frac{150}{3}$ = 50
    50 × two teams exactly ratio of 2 = 100
2.   B
    The ratio is 5 : 1. Add the ratios to get 6.
    360 degrees in a pie chart so $\frac{360}{6}$ = 60
    60 × pants ratio of 1 = 60 degrees

Pages 18–19

Challenge 1
a)   40 cm
    Perimeter = 10 cm × 4 equal sides of the square = 40 cm
b)   28 cm
    Perimeter = (2 × 6 cm sides) + (2 × 8 cm sides) = 28 cm
c)   64 cm
    Perimeter = 8 + 24 + 8 + 24 = 64 cm

Challenge 2
a) 49 cm²   b) 108 cm²   c) 66 cm²

Challenge 3

Width	Length	Perimeter	Area
20 cm	20 cm	**80 cm**	400 cm²
15 cm	25 cm	80 cm	**375 cm²**
10 cm	**20 cm**	60 cm	200 cm²
100 cm	**150 cm**	500 cm	**15,000 cm²**

Challenge 4
a) 104 cm

Perimeter = 30 + 22 + 17 + 13 = 82 + the two unknown sides. Find the sides from the other lengths, so (30 – 17) = 13 and (22 – 13) = 9, so 82 + 13 + 9 = 104

b) 543 cm²

To find area, break down into two rectangles, so (30 × 13) = 390, (17 × 9) = 153
390 + 153 = 543 cm²

Now Try This!
1. D

If square has a perimeter of 60 cm, then width = $\frac{60}{4}$ = 15 cm
So Donna's square = 30 cm × 30 cm = 900 cm²

2. A

Right-angled triangle, so area = $\frac{(6 \times 16)}{2}$ = 48 cm²

Pages 20–21
Challenge 1
a) 60 degrees

Equilateral triangle means all the angles are the same, so $\frac{180}{3}$ = 60 degrees

b) 84 degrees

180 degrees in a triangle, so 180 – 48 – 48 = 84 degrees

c) Isosceles

Two angles are the same size, so it is an isosceles triangle.

Challenge 2
a) 52 degrees

180 degrees on a straight line, so the missing bottom right angle of the triangle is:
180 – 63 – 49 = 68 degrees
So angle x is:
180 – 60 – 68 = 52 degrees

b) 180 degrees

Cutting the square in half makes two triangles, so 180 degrees.

Challenge 3
a)

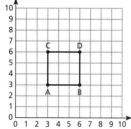

b) (6, 9)

Translating by (3, 3) means moving 3 across and 3 up so (6, 9).

c)

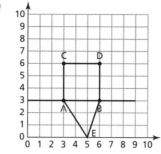

d) (5, 6)

Challenge 4
a) Square-based pyramid
b) Cone

Now Try This!
1. D

Isosceles triangle has two identical angles, so if 70 is the biggest then the other two must be $\frac{110}{2}$ = 55 degrees

2. D

Paula: radius 50 cm, diameter 100 cm
Jack: radius 100 cm, diameter 200 cm
Dave: radius 200 cm, diameter 400 cm

Pages 22–23
Challenge 1
a) $y = 13$ b) $x = 5$ c) $x = 7$
d) $y = 5$ e) $y = 3$ f) $x = 10$

Challenge 2
a) $y = 8$

$5x + y = 38$, $(5 \times 6) + y = 38$, $30 + y = 38$
$y = 38 – 30$, $y = 8$

b) $y = 4.5$

$15x = 4y + 72$, $(15 \times 6) = 4y + 72$, $90 = 4y + 72$
$18 = 4y$, $y = 4.5$

c) $x = 21$

$(5 \times 8) + 7 = 26 + x$, $47 = 26 + x$, $x = 21$

d) $x = 14$

$(7 + 8) – x = 1$, $15 – x = 1$, $x = 14$

e) $y = 2$

$(2 \times -4) = -10 + y$, $-8 = -10 + y$, $y = 2$

f) $y = -5$

$-15 – -4 = -16 – y$, $-15 + 4 = -16 – y$
$-11 = -16 – y$, $5 = -y$, $y = -5$

Challenge 3
a) $x = 7$

$9x – 30 = 2x + 19$
$7x = 49$, $x = 7$

b) $y = 2$

$14y^2 = 56$, $14(y^2) = 56$
So $y^2 = 4$, $y = 2$

c) $x = 5$

$\frac{50}{x} = 2x$, $50 = 2x^2$, $x = 5$

d) $y = 1$

$35y^2 = 35$, $y = 1$

Challenge 4
a) $y = 5$

$3 + 2x(y + 1) = 27$, $3 + 4(y + 1) = 27$,
$3 + 4y + 4 = 27$
$4y = 20$, $y = 5$

b) $y = 1$

$29 + 3x(y + 7) = 77$, $29 + 6(y + 7) = 77$,
$29 + 6y + 42 = 77$
$6y = 6$, $y = 1$

c) $y = 3$

$(16 \times 9) + 16 + 9y = 190 – y$, $144 + 16 + 9y = 190 – y$, $160 + 9y = 190 – y$, $10y = 30$,
$y = 3$

d) $y = 9$

$(9^2 + 25) + 2y = 133 – y$, $106 + 2y = 133 – y$, $3y = 27$, $y = 9$

Now Try This!
1. B

It is $4(6y + 3) = 24y + 12$

2. B

It is $2(2x + y) + 2(7x + 2y) =$
$4x + 2y + 14x + 4y$
$= 18x + 6y$

Pages 24–25
Challenge 1
a) 30p

$4R + 3P = 2.90$, so $4(0.5) + 3P = 2.90$,
$2 + 3P = 2.90$
$3P = 0.90$, $P = 30p$

b) $4x + 3y = 12.50$

c) 50p

$4C + 3B = 6.50$, $4C + 3(1.5) = 6.5$,
$4C + 4.50 = 6.5$, $4C = 2$, $C = 50p$

d) $18x = 11$

Challenge 2
a) $y = 2$

$7y + x = 29$, so $7y + 15 = 29$
$7y = 14$, $y = 2$

b) $y = 1$

$12y + 2x = 30$, so $12y + 2(9) = 30$,
$12y + 18 = 30$
$12y = 12$, $y = 1$

c) $y = 2$

$22y + 4(13) = 96$, $22y + 52 = 96$,
$22y = 44$, $y = 2$

d) $y = 60$

$300 – y – 3(50) = 90$, $300 – y – 150 = 90$,
$150 – y = 90$, $y = 60$

Challenge 3
a) i) $8x + 6y = 4.20$
   ii) $8x + 2y = 14.50$
b) i) $15y + 9x = 36$
   ii) $3y + 12x = 63$
c) $2x = 3.50$

$(7y + 3x = 7.50) – (7y + x = 4)$ is $2x = 3.50$

d) $8y + 4x = 18$

$(20y + 10x = 45) – (12y + 6x = 27)$ is
$8y + 4x = 18$

Challenge 4
a) $x = 1, y = 0.5$

Multiply second equation by 2 to get
$4x + 6y = 7$
Subtract first equation from that to get
$4y = 2$
So $4y = 2$, $y = 0.5$
Put into original equation to get
$4x + 2(0.5) = 5$
$4x = 4$, $x = 1$
So $x = 1, y = 0.5$

b) $x = 0.8, y = 1.25$

Double the first equation to get
$6x + 4y = 9.8$; subtract second equation to get $2x = 1.60$, $x = 0.8$
Substitute into first equation to get
$3(0.8) + 2y = 4.90$, $2.4 + 2y = 4.9$,
$2y = 2.5$, $y = 1.25$

c) $x = 1.05, y = 1.30$

Double second equation to get
$10x + 4y = 15.7$; subtract first equation to get $7x = 7.35$, $x = 1.05$
Substitute into first equation to get
$3(1.05) + 4y = 8.35$, $3.15 + 4y = 8.35$,
$4y = 5.2$, $y = 1.30$

Now Try This!
1. **B**
   3S + 4F = 8.50
   6S + 5F = 14
   So double first equation to get
   6S + 8F = 17
   Subtract second equation to get 3F = 3,
   F = 1
   Put in original equation to get
   3S + 4(1) = 8.50, 3S = 4.50, S = £1.50
   So 1 stapler = £1.50, 1 folder = £1
2. **B**
   4R + 3C = 4.10
   3R + 6C = 5.70
   Double first equation to get 8R + 6C = 8.20
   Subtract second equation to get 5R = 2.50, R = 50p
   Put in first equation to get 4(0.5) + 3C = 4.10, 2 + 3C = 4.10, 3C = 2.10, C = 70p
   So 1 kitchen roll = 50p, 1 cheese slice = 70p

Pages 26–27
Challenge 1
a) 12
   Mean = $\frac{(7 + 14 + 14 + 21 + 4)}{5}$ = 12
b) 14
   Mode is the most common value, so 14.
c) 17
   Range = 21 − 4 = 17
d) 14
   Median is the middle value when ordered to 4, 7, 14, 14, 21
e) 34
   34 − 4 = 30

Challenge 2
a) 0
b) 11
   Mean = $\frac{(16 + 0 + 0 + 32 + 12 + 6)}{6}$ = 11
c) 9
   Values when ordered are 0, 0, 6, 12, 16, 32
   Median = $\frac{(6 + 12)}{2}$ = 9
d) 32
   32 − 0 = 32
e) 13
   16 + 0 + 0 + 44 + 12 + 6 = 78
   $\frac{78}{6}$ = 13
f) 44
   44 − 0 = 44
g) 9
   Values when ordered are 0, 0, 6, 12, 16, 44
   Median = $\frac{(6 + 12)}{2}$ = 9

Challenge 3
a) 25
   25 is the most common number of stickers.
b) 25
   When ordered, the data values are 10, 15, 25, 25, 25
c) 15
   25 − 10 = 15
d) 20
   $\frac{(10 + 15 + 25 + 25 + 25)}{5}$ = 20

Challenge 4
a) 11
   14 − 3 = 11
b) 18
   Mode = 3, median = 7, mean = 8
   3 + 7 + 8 = 18

Now Try This!
1. **B**
   After 7 results the mean will be 66.
   That must mean her total marks would have been 66 × 7 = 462. So 462 − 82 − 44 − 73 − 49 − 65 − 71 = 78
2. **E**
   If a, b, c have a mode of 15 then both b and c must be 15. A mean of 13 means the total of a + b + c = 39 as $\frac{39}{3}$ = 13, so 39 − 15 − 15 = 9. Therefore a + b = 9 + 15 = 24

Pages 28–29
Challenge 1
a)
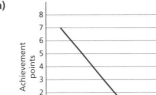
b) 12
   7 + 4 + 1 = 12
c) 6
   7 − 1 = 6

Challenge 2
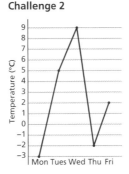

Challenge 3

Colour	Number	Size of pie chart angle
Black	50	90°
Red	100	180°
Green	50	90°

Challenge 4
a) 48
   The given percentages add up to 30 + 34 + 24 = 88, so netball must be 12%
   12% is half of 24% so $\frac{96}{2}$ = 48
b) 400
   If 96 = 24% then $\frac{96}{x} = \frac{24}{100}$, $\frac{9,600}{x}$ = 24, x = 400

Now Try This!
1. **C**
   So $\frac{2}{5}$ are not looking at their phone.
   $\frac{1}{5}$ therefore looking out of the window.
   $\frac{1}{5}$ × 360 = 72 degrees

2. **A**
   360 : 240 = 3 : 2 ratio. Add ratios to get 5. $\frac{360}{5}$ = 72
   72 × 2 = 144 degrees

Pages 30–33
1. a) 24
   Prime factors of 8 = 2 × 2 × 2
   Prime factors of 6 = 2 × 3
   2 × 2 × 2 × 3 = 24
   b) 6
   Factors of 12 are 1, 2, 3, 4, 6, 12
   Factors of 18 are 1, 2, 3, 6, 9, 18
   So highest common factor is 6
2. a) 1 hour 26 minutes
   12:08 to 13:34 = 1 hour 26 minutes
   b) 18:29
   27 minutes later than 18:02 is 18:29
3. a) Town B
   b) 75 miles
   c) 45 miles
   Town B is 22 miles from Town A and Town D is 67 miles from Town A.
   67 − 22 = 45 miles
4. a) 34
   Adding 5 each time
   b) 7
   Subtracting by 1 more each time
   c) 88
   Adding the two previous numbers
5. a) (2, −4)
   b) (2, 2)
6. 7.5 km
   10 km/h = $\frac{10}{60}$ per minute = $\frac{1}{6}$ per minute
   36 × $\frac{1}{6}$ = $\frac{36}{6}$ = 6 km
   5 km/h = $\frac{5}{60}$ per minute = $\frac{1}{12}$ per minute
   18 × $\frac{1}{12}$ = 1.5 km, so 6 + 1.5 = 7.5 km
7. a) 120 degrees
   There are 60 minutes in an hour and 360 degrees in a circle, so each minute is $\frac{360}{60}$ = 6 degrees. At 4:00 there will be 20 minutes between the hands, so 120 degrees.
   b) 105 degrees
   At 2:30 the hour hand will be halfway between 2 and 3, so there will be 17.5 minutes between them. 17.5 × 6 = 105 degrees
8. a) (5, 1)
   b) (−2, 2)

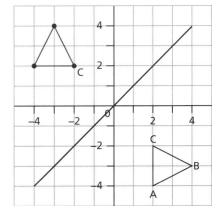

9. 2.5 miles

   He is going for 30 minutes at 5 mph.

   $\frac{30}{60} = 0.5$

   $0.5 \times 5 = 2.5$ miles

10. $\frac{1}{8}$

    Probability of a head with one toss of the coin is $\frac{1}{2}$

    $\frac{1}{2} \times \frac{1}{2} \times \frac{1}{2} = \frac{1}{8}$

11. a) 50%

       1, 3, 5, 7, 9, 11, 13, 15, 17, 19 = 10 numbers

       $\frac{10}{20} = 50\%$

    b) 10%

       1, 5

       $\frac{2}{20}$ so 10%

    c) 80%

       1, 4, 9, 16 are square numbers, so

       $\frac{16}{20}$ so 80%

    d) 40%

       2, 3, 5, 7, 11, 13, 17, 19

       $\frac{8}{20}$ so 40%

12. a) East

    b) South West

Verbal Ability Activities

Pages 34–35
Challenge 1

a) Various answers are possible. Answers may include comments about an atmosphere of disappointment or tension as William does not know what to bring his children and cannot think of something that will make them happy. *(1 mark for the selection of a suitable quotation and 2 marks for analysis of the effect of the quotation)*

b) We would expect the children to be happy when they are bought sweets, but they are ungrateful *(1 mark)*. Therefore, there is contrast between the children's disappointment about the colour of the ribbons and the repetition of the gifts and what we would expect them to feel *(1 mark)*.

c) William means that the question of what to bring his children as a present cannot be answered easily *(1 mark)*, as they do not like the sweets and he cannot go to the toyshop any more *(1 mark)*.

Challenge 2

a) Mrs Saville evidently feels that the narrator's journey is a foolish undertaking *(1 mark)* and things will not go well ('an enterprise which you have regarded with such evil forebodings') *(1 mark)*.

b) Mrs Margaret Saville

c) The writer feels that things are going well and the journey will be successful *(1 mark)*. As time goes on, the writer feels more and more certain that they will accomplish what they set out to do *(1 mark)*.

d) The writer has gone to St Petersburgh.

e) The writer feels invigorated and captivated by the weather ('braces my nerves, and fills me with delight'). *(1 mark for the explanation and 1 mark for the quotation)*

f) The writer tries unsuccessfully *(1 mark)* to convince himself that the North Pole and the surrounding regions are unpleasant and sorrowful *(1 mark)*; however, the landscape actually captures his imagination and makes him feel inventive and invigorated *(1 mark)*.

g) The people who have ventured over this landscape before the narrator.

h) Various answers are possible. Answers could include comment on a bleak, ominous atmosphere. The narrator's upbeat attitude seems unfounded as the landscape is cold and harsh. However, there is an ambiguity about what will happen: answers could hint at a positive attitude/atmosphere as the narrator is convinced it will go well. *[The strongest candidates will use a P-E-A structure (a <u>point</u> made in their own words, followed by supporting <u>evidence</u> in the form of a quotation from the passage, then an <u>analytical</u> section explaining in greater detail). Each section of the PEA answer scores 1 mark (no marks for repetition of the evidence without a candidate's own words).]*

Now Try This!

C There is much scandal as it is a tantalising story

We are told that there is 'intense interest' and the case is notorious. There are 'sensational rumours', which indicates that people are still interested in what had happened.

Pages 36–37
Challenge 1

a) Dorian wonders whether looking at the picture will start to show the unpleasant aspects of his character *[1 mark]* and make him start to think he is an uncaring, unkind person *[1 mark]*.

b) The writer uses personification to suggest that the eyes of the portrait 'follow' Dorian around as he looks at it *[1 mark]*. This creates an unsettling atmosphere that makes Dorian feel ill at ease *[1 mark]*.

c) Dorian feels guilty about how he has treated Sybil Vane extremely badly in the past *[1 mark]* and now thinks he needs to apologise to her *[1 mark]*. He feels that if he does this, he can fall in love with her again and they will be happy once more *[1 mark]*.

d) At the end of the passage, the lovely weather mimics Dorian's good intentions towards Sybil *[1 mark]* and suggests that the idyllic landscape outside will be similar to the idyllic way Dorian thinks of his relationship with Sybil *[1 mark]*.

Challenge 2

Answers will vary. *[5 marks per mind map]*

Challenge 3

a) Seeing the man has made the narrator stop in his tracks *[1 mark]* and surprised him *[1 mark]*.

b) The man is extremely tall *[1 mark]*; he has a 'careless powerful look' which makes him seem imposing *[1 mark]*; he has a problem with his legs or feet which means he walks with a limp *[1 mark]*; he has a 'bleak and unapproachable' face which suggests he has a miserable and off-putting expression *[1 mark]*; he is very stiff and does not move easily *[1 mark]*; he looks much older than he really is *[1 mark]*.

c) The local people are tall and thin (they are described in the text as having 'lank longitude').

d) i) 'Lameness checking each step like the jerk of a chain'

   ii) This makes it seem as though the limp makes each step fractured and jerky, as though the man has been tied up like livestock with a strong chain *[1 mark]*, causing him great difficulty in walking *[1 mark]*.

Now Try This!

A All of the hosts appear anonymous and homogenous.

Some of the hosts are reduced to 'Miss This-or-That' and we don't hear anything about the other hosts except their names, making them two-dimensional and flat.

Pages 38–39
Challenge 1

[1 mark for correct identification of the technique and up to 2 marks for analysis of the effects created]

a) The writer uses a metaphor to suggest the sea is like a house with a basement that has mythical creatures in it and is therefore exciting, mysterious and somehow magical.

b) The writer uses alliteration to suggest that the ropes of the boats are extending like hands towards the narrator, creating a welcoming atmosphere. *[Also accept any suitable answer which identifies the use of metaphor and its effect]*

c) The writer uses repetition to mimic the washing of the tide sweeping past the narrator and exaggerating the immersive effect of the narrator standing in the water as the tide comes in.

d) The writer uses personification to make the sea seem as though it is courteous, waving the narrator farewell as the tide goes out. Thus, it seems as though the narrator has had a very personal relationship with the sea as it withdraws.

Challenge 2

a) The town of Mayenfeld is picturesque, situated amongst the valleys and peaks of the Alps *[1 mark]*. The surrounding plants are fragrant and smell lovely *[1 mark]*. The mountains overshadow the town and a footpath leads upwards into the mountains *[1 mark]*.

b) **Any from:** The little girl has rosy cheeks; she has a sun-tan; she is wrapped up in lots of clothing (two dresses and a shawl and probably other layers); she is about five years old; she has stout boots on; she is too hot; she is walking arduously up the mountain. *[The strongest candidates will use a P-E-A structure (a point made in their own words, followed by supporting evidence in the form of a quotation from the passage, then an analytical section explaining in greater detail). Each section of the PEA answer scores 1 mark (no marks for repetition of the evidence without a candidate's own words).]*

c) Alm-Uncle is an unusual character (not like 'other mortals') and seems poorly suited to looking after a child *[1 mark]*. He is not necessarily easy to get along with ('She'll never get along with him, I am sure of that!') *[1 mark]*.

d) She means 'tell me about what you're doing'

e) Deta is going to become a housekeeper for some people in Frankfurt *[1 mark]* and work in a smart house for people who were previously very happy with her work *[1 mark]*.

Now Try This!
B He is elusive and secretive.
Basil Hallward is shown in the extract to be wondering where Dorian might have got to the previous evening and felt 'miserable' at not finding Dorian.

Pages 40–41
Challenge 1
a) receipt   b) yield
c) fierce   d) beige
Challenge 2
a) **im**practical   b) **ir**resolute
c) **in**definite   d) **de**compose
e) **un**even   f) **ir**respective
g) **dis**trust / **mis**trust   h) **il**legal
Challenge 3
a)   i) reign   ii) alter   iii) bare
    iv) dissent   v) practise
b)   i) edition   ii) precede   iii) except
    iv) lightning   v) excess   vi) dessert
Challenge 4
a) geese   b) trout   c) diagnoses
d) ellipses   e) quizzes   f) series
g) leaves   h) oxen   i) aircraft
Now Try This!
1. a) D
      The correct spelling is 'correspondent'.
   b) E
      The correct spelling is 'psychological'.
2. a) parl**ia**ment   b) desperate
   c) nuis**a**nce   d) privilege

Pages 42–43
Challenge 1
a) <u>Buckingham Palace</u> is one of London's most popular tourist attractions.   **PN**
b) <u>The amazing acrobats</u> thrilled us with their breathtaking acts.   **NP**

c) <u>Looking around him, he</u> was certain he'd been here before.   P
d) "Please will <u>you</u> call an electrician?"   P
e) <u>Hailstones</u> pounded the caravan roof as we cooked our breakfast.   N

Challenge 2
a) A group of Year 6 children **is** / was representing the school at the debate.
b) Mum said me and my sister are / **were** allowed to go into town on our bikes tomorrow.
c) If I **were** to win a million pounds, I'd cruise around the Caribbean.
d) Should you **be** cold, please turn on the heating.

Challenge 3
A few years ago, we **decided** to go camping. It **was** our first time and I must say, we **were** very excited. Little **did** we know that it **was** going to rain the entire time! However, I wouldn't say it **ruined** our trip – we **were** able to spend the evenings in the recreation room where we **played** table tennis and **met** lots of new friends. We also **swam** in the lake and **built** dens in the forest.

Challenge 4
Noun: discovery
Adjective: ancient
Verb: was
Adverbial phrase: Last night
Preposition: on
Pronoun: he
Now Try This!
1. B   her
2. C   adverb
3. E   adjective

Pages 44–45
Challenge 1
Answers will vary.
Word: clemency
Meaning: Act of mercy towards someone who has committed a crime.
Word in a sentence: The judge showed clemency towards the offender by only imprisoning him for 2 years.

Word: gregarious
Meaning: Describes someone who likes being with people.
Word in a sentence: Theo is a lively, gregarious person who enjoys social events.

Word: meticulous
Meaning: Describes someone who shows great attention to detail.
Word in a sentence: After hours of meticulous preparation, we finished our amazing art display on the classroom wall.

Word: Wholesome
Meaning: Describes something that is good for you.
Word in a sentence: A wholesome breakfast before leaving the house will stand you in good stead for the morning.

Challenge 2
a) scrub
b) anticipate
c) superfluous
d) unorthodox

Challenge 3
a) wound   gash
b) subterfuge   trick
c) painstaking   meticulous
d) adhere   bind

Challenge 4
Lines drawn as follows:

a)	sentry	to	A soldier who guards something
b)	innocuous	to	Something that is harmless
c)	meagre	to	A very small amount/not enough of something
d)	omen	to	An event thought to tell what will happen in the future

Now Try This!
1. D   skilled
    'Accomplished' means to be skilful or expert at something.
2. B   disobey
    'Defy' means to refuse to obey or go against someone.

Pages 46–47
Challenge 1
Answers will vary. Examples:
a) We saw a great film last night.
b) The carpenter used a saw to cut the wood.
c) A clog is a type of shoe made from wood.
d) If you pour grease down the sink, it may clog up the pipe.
e) Mum chose nursing as her career.
f) The truck lost control and began to career down the road.

Challenge 2
a) rushed
    The others suggest moving slowly, whereas the 'urgent' ring of the bell implies Robert would rush.
b) immobilise
    The others mean deploying the missile, which would not avoid an international crisis.
c) frogs
    The others are not amphibians.
d) Somalia
    The others are continents, not countries.

Challenge 3
a) coal
    The others are wood.
b) mine
    They are all possessive pronouns but 'mine' can also be a noun or a verb related to excavation.
c) excavate
    The others relate to looking for something.
d) quarry
    The others relate to hiding something.
e) coal
    Mine, excavate and quarry all relate to how you would *obtain* coal.

Challenge 4
a) D   thorough though
    The other words are prepositions. 'thorough' is an adjective and 'though' is a subordinating conjunction.

b) **B** bridle isle

The rest are associated with a wedding. The homophone 'bridle' can be a set of leather straps around a horse's head (noun) or to react in anger (verb); 'isle' is a homophone of 'aisle' (which might be associated with a church wedding).

c) **C** bank deposit

'Bank' and 'deposit' as verbs can mean to place money with a bank. The other words all relate to supporting someone or something.

Now Try This!

1. **A** conceive

'Conceive' means to imagine; the others mean to confuse.

2. **E** centipede

A centipede has more than six legs/is an arthropod, whereas the others have six legs/are insects.

3. **D** zodiac

'Zodiac' is associated with astrology whereas the others are associated with astronomy.

Pages 48–49
Challenge 1
Answers will vary. Examples:

	A sentence that uses the word as a noun	A sentence that uses the word as a verb
bark	I touched the rough bark of the tree.	Cal heard the dog bark in the night.
address	Shay wrote his address on the letter.	The politician will address the audience later.
stem	The stem holds up the flower of a plant.	The doctor tried to stem the bleeding.

Challenge 2
a) As the troops <u>approached</u> the besieged city, the panicked inhabitants <u>retreated</u> into their homes.

b) The silversmith expertly fashioned a <u>delicate</u> flower pendant, each with exceptionally <u>fragile</u> petals.

c) i) optimistic
   ii) bizarre

Challenge 3
a) dissent   acceptance
b) fascination   disinterest
c) secrete   expose
d) superior   subordinate

Challenge 4
a) **Fragile** is to **robust** as **faint** is to **strong**.
b) **Contract** is to **shrink** as **shrivel** is to **diminish**.
c) **Ample** is to **plenty** as **meagre** is to **insufficient**.
d) **Resolute** is to **determined** as **timid** is to **fainthearted**.

Now Try This!
1. **B** flog
2. **C** vulnerable

Pages 50–51
Challenge 1
a) disguise   b) tree   c) never
d) Birds   e) stitch   f) penny

Challenge 2
a) join   seam
b) screen   monitor
c) wrist   knee
d) Earth   Jupiter

Challenge 3
Lines should be drawn as follows:
ornate   to   decorative   intricate
intent   to   determined   aim
prominent   to   famous   noticeable
tender   to   give or offer gentle

Challenge 4
a) state
b) range
c) cast
d) rough

Now Try This!
1. **E** wind

The idiom 'throw caution to the wind', meaning to act recklessly.

2. **A** sad

The expression 'to feel blue', meaning to feel sad.

3. **E** speak

The verb 'orate', meaning to make a speech.

Pages 52–53
Challenge 1
a) **B** lose, while
b) **C** was, all
c) **E** Despite, with
d) **D** at, struggle

Challenge 2
a) assassinated
b) unpronounced
c) potent
d) precipitating

Challenge 3
The Giant's Causeway on the Antrim coast of Northern Ireland was formed around 60 million years ago, during the Paleogene Period. It was an area of [**H** intense] volcanic [**E** activity] which resulted in [**L** successive] flows of lava [**G** inching] toward the coast and [**F** cooling] when they reached the Atlantic Ocean.

The Giant's Causeway is made [**I** up] of around 40,000 basalt columns tumbling down to the sea. These hexagonal-shaped [**J** stepping] stones in an area of stunning [**K** natural] beauty attract thousands of tourists every year.

Legend [**D** has] it that the Giant's Causeway was built [**B** by] the Irish giant, Finn MacCool, as a crossing to [**C** confront] his Scottish rival, the giant Benandonner. Arriving in Ireland for the fight, Benandonner was so [**A** frightened] at the sight of the massive Irish giant that he ran back to Scotland, ripping up the stones as he went.

Now Try This!
Question 1: **D**   Question 2: **E**
Question 3: **C**   Question 4: **B**
Question 5: **A**

Pages 54–55
Challenge 1

				1i		2v	
		4d	e	s	c	e	n	3t
			i		l		i	
5v		s		e		n		r
a		s			6b			e
7a	i	s	l	e		8b	o	a	r
n			n			r		
		9t	y	r	e		

Challenge 2

Subject	Verb	Adjective	Noun	Adverb
the vet	treated	injured	rabbit	carefully
he/Val	returned	forgetful	owner	always
we	is	lucky	birthday	hard
Ethan	remembers	caring	teachers	later
	are	excellent	lessons	
	work	older	idea	
	deliver		cousin	
	has			
	is coming			
	surprise			

[*Also accept the following in the Noun column: 'Val', 'Vikrum' and 'Ethan' (proper nouns) and 'the vet'.*]

Challenge 3
a) On Saturday night, we usually have a takeaway.
b) My mum likes watching comedies and quiz shows. / My mum likes watching quiz shows and comedies.
c) In the blink of an eye, the prince was turned into a frog. / In the blink of an eye, the frog was turned into a prince.
d) Absence makes the heart grow fonder.

Challenge 4
It's been such a long time since we saw our grandparents. They live on the coast in a small cottage which has a view of the sea. My gran is an artist and she encourages me to paint. When I walk through the door to her studio, I am transported to another world!
Shuffled sentence: *has the safe she the key to*
Correct order: *She has the key to the safe.*

Now Try This!
1. **D** post

The striker put the ball in the net.

2. **B** raining

Flooding has caused havoc on the east coast.

3. **C** it

You can't judge a book by its cover.

Pages 56–61
1. **C**

We are told that his smile reaches almost from ear to ear, and that his eyes crinkle up when he smiles. The overall effect of his smile is compared to a drawing of the sun shining.

2. **C**

We are told that for Gabriel there are six times as many working days as Sundays.

3. **D**

Overall he is wearing clothes that are suitable for spending much of the day outside – even in a river – in comfort and that have been well-made specifically for that purpose.

4. **B**
Legs and feet; we are told that he has 'leather leggings' and shoes on them.

5. **A**
We are told that they have been made for practical reasons but that they have not been cut for aesthetics.

6. **B**
The watch is the size of a small clock, has unreliable timekeeping and is inconvenient to use.

7. **A**
We are told that Gabriel uses his watch and the 'sun and stars' as well as peeping through the windows of people's houses to tell the time.

8. **B**
It is a simile 'like a bucket from a well'.

9. **B**
Gabriel's youthfulness has not yet left his face and body.

10. **D**
We are told that he is tall and physically broad, which could appear threatening or imposing to people if Gabriel wants to.

11. **B**
Noun

12. **C**
Perceive

13. **D**
Considered

14. **A**
Adjective

15. The Owl and the Pussy-cat went to sea   **free**
In a beautiful pea-green boat,   **float**
They took some honey, and plenty of money,   **take**
Wrapped up in a five-pound note.   **coat**

16. a) adversary   ring
   b) Due to   ascent
17. a) delicate   obscure
   b) specific   tasty
18. a) spot
   b) function
19. a) c o u n c i l   b) p r o c e **d** u r e
   c) c a f f **e** i n e   d) p r e c o c **i o** u s
20. a) wrong   b) killed
   c) blue   d) glitters
21. a) love
     It is the only positive emotion.
   b) lovely
     The others are adverbs.
   c) chameleon
     The others are mammals.
   d) hilarious
     The others mean very silly/stupid.
22. a) sapphire   ruby
   b) amiable   genial
23. While I was young I **lived** upon my mother's milk, as I could not eat grass. In the daytime I ran by her side, and **at** night I **lay** down close **by** her. When it was **hot** we used to **stand** by the **pond** in the **shade** of the trees, and when it was **cold** we had a nice warm **shed** near the **plantation**.
24. a) bag   kindling
     The others relate to getting rid of someone from their job.

---

   b) sparse   meagre
     The others describe something that is fancy or very detailed.
25. a) A   possible
   b) C   inseparably
26. a) C   preposition
   b) B   adjective

Non-Verbal Ability Activities
Pages 62–63
Challenge 1
Drawings should include all of the features listed.
a) The figures have the following in common:
- Rectangular shape
- Divided into triangles the same shape
- Patterns made up of four small shapes, which are repeated at either end of each rectangle

b) The figures have the following in common:
- Same overall area
- Divided into six equal sections
- Two black dots in one section, a cross in two sections, a circle in one section

c) All of the figures are made up of the same shape with just the position of the two dots and the colours changing.

Challenge 2
a) A, W, V, T, M have only vertical symmetry; B, E, K, C, D have only horizontal symmetry; H, I, O have both horizontal and vertical symmetry.
b) S is the odd one out as it has no symmetry.

Challenge 3
a) i) The square fields are similar as they have all been divided with three straight lines to create four spaces.
   ii) Any suitable answer, e.g. The odd one out could be A as it is the only field with three quadrilaterals created.
b) i) The rectangular fields are similar as they have all been divided with three straight lines.
   ii) F: could be the odd one out because it is the only field with a pentagon as one of the sub-sections
G: could be the odd one out because it is the only field with one sub-section taking up exactly half
I: could be the odd one out because it is the only field with divisions that cross over one another

Now Try This!
1. a) **B**
     The images on the left all show arrows going clockwise, with a black dot on the section before the arrowhead.
   b) **A**
     The images on the left are all made up of seven lines and have a vertical line of symmetry.
2. a) **C**
     The only option with two diagonal lines on faces.

---

   b) **E**
     The only option with the circles touching different sides of the semicircle and cutting across the semicircle, rather than both touching the same side of the semicircle around the edge as in all the other figures.

Pages 64–65
Challenge 1
a) i) They have been reflected.
   ii) Dot added on top and pole no longer visible in rectangle of the boat.
   iii) White triangles have disappeared.
b) i) Large red sail has moved across to the right-hand side of the boat.
   ii) The pink section is divided into two not three; the stripes have changed from horizontal to vertical.
c) i) Dot added on top.
   ii) The flag is to the left of the flagpole rather than to the right; division has swapped from diagonal to horizontal; scallops have changed to zigzags.
   iii) Bold line has disappeared; small blue triangles at the top have been added; triangles at the sides have been merged with the boat; horizontal dividing line has appeared.

Challenge 2
a) Answer should include: fish becomes smaller; two concentric triangles in the tail; seven scallops in the tail; three gill lines each side.
b) Answer should include: fish rotated 90 degrees anticlockwise; six perpendicular lines on tail; four squares with circles inside them; crossed lines on fish's body.

Challenge 3
a) **D**
Each fish gains two bubbles and the seaweed appears.
b) **B**
The coral gains two extra branches and one extra dot.

Now Try This!
1. **E**
Each image moves one place anticlockwise around the edge.
2. **D**
The second image is the mirror image of the first.

Pages 66–67
Challenge 1
a) The missing tile should have the blue square in it, with a diagonal line going from bottom left to top right.
b) The pattern runs diagonally from top left to bottom right. The number of stars stays the same and the diagonal black line alternates positions. The missing tile should look like the one directly above it, except with one + sign rather than two.
c) The missing tile should have a heavy black line on the right. In the middle

---

there should be a rectangle with a black dot in the bottom half.

d) The missing tile should have a green rectangle in the top left-hand corner and a green L-shape in the bottom right-hand corner. The solid vertical line should move to the left-hand side. The wavy line should move upwards in the tile. There should be a double > shape in the centre.

Challenge 2
Answers should reflect the following rules:

a) Moving anti-clockwise around the hexagons, the small shapes move two segments anti-clockwise each time.

b) The scalloped and fine line should continue on the diagonal. There should be three short lines across the left-hand outer edge of the hexagon. There should be three black circles and three open circles.

c) Moving clockwise around the outer hexagons, the number of dots alternates between 1, 2, 3. The striped wedge moves one place clockwise around the small hexagons each time. The double ended arrow alternates between being horizontal and vertical. The parallel lines move two places anticlockwise around the sides of the hexagons each time.

Challenge 3
Each octagon is a 180-degree rotation of the octagon directly opposite. In the centre of the grid, there is a small asterisk in the innermost point of the triangle and alternating bold or fine lines with matching bold or fine crosses.

Now Try This!
1. A
   Moving from left to right, the polygons change shape as the shading rotates 90 degrees. The polygons gain an extra side from left to right.
2. C
   The missing tile should be the same as that in the centre of the top row, reflected in a horizontal mirror line.
3. B
   The missing tile should have a hexagon reflected in a horizontal mirror line (so it would not change from the bottom left of the grid), the arrow having swapped direction and the dashed line having moved inside the polygon at the top.

Pages 68–69
Challenge 1
a) Top and bottom rows flow together: moving from left to right, the black square moves one section clockwise each time; the clover alternates between the top right-hand square (top row) and the right-hand triangle (bottom row).

b) Top and bottom rows flow together: moving from left to right, the V-shape moves from left to right. Top row: the bold short line is horizontal. Arrows mirror each other from one figure to the next. Arrowheads consistent (all bold). Bottom row: the bold short line

is vertical. Arrows mirror each other in one figure to the next. Arrowheads consistent (all open).

Challenge 2
a) All the figures in blue are the same, so the answer should be identical to other blue figures.

b) The answer should have a heavy black stripe at the bottom, dashes that fit the sequence (they are reducing in size with each pink triangle) and four scallops.

c) The answer should have horizontal shading to the right of the vertical line, three black squares on the left-hand side of the vertical line and a small open square with a line through the top left corner.

Challenge 3
Answers will vary.

Now Try This!
1. B
   Moving from left to right, the V-shape moves gradually clockwise around the circle and one additional scallop is added. The horizontal line rises up the square from left to right.
2. E
   Moving from left to right, each line becomes gradually thicker and the pattern continues as new fine lines are added.
3. C
   Moving from left to right, the number of black dots increases by 1. The curved line moves from left to right in each square. The bold lines at the bottom of each square alternate between a cross, an L-shape and a T-shape, and back again.
4. B
   Moving from left to right, the bold lines alternate between low and high; the dots increase in number from 1 to 3 and start again; the crosses turn one at a time to a circle and then disappear.

Pages 70–71
Challenge 1
Answers as follows from the top of page 70:
LO
(E = heart positioned outside the rectangle; L = heart positioned inside the rectangle; O = fine vertical line; J = bold vertical line)
OK
(O = dot below the curved line; G = no dot; C = dot above the curved line; N = diagonal cross inside purple box; K = vertical/ horizontal cross inside purple box; C = horizontal stripes inside purple box)
BY
(U = fine diagonal line goes from top left to bottom middle; B = fine diagonal line goes from bottom left to top middle; R = fine horizontal line is below the bold horizontal line; Y = fine horizontal line is above the bold horizontal line)
PO
(R = three pairs of branches; P = four pairs of branches; S = five pairs of branches; Q = trapezium pot; X = square pot; O = rectangular pot)

ST
(X = bold outline; S = 'bubble writing' outline; Y = dashed outline; A = no symmetry; Z = horizontal symmetry only; T = vertical and horizontal symmetry)
BO
(C = triangles arranged so that they touch at a point; B = triangles arranged so they touch by a side; P = dots touching like a flower; Q = dots vertical; O = dots diagonal)
XN
(E = black rectangle; F = rectangle black at either end and open in the middle; H = open rectangle; X = rectangle open at either end and black in the middle; R = blue rectangle equally divided into four; N = blue rectangle divided into 2 upper sections and 3 lower ones; T = blue rectangle divided into 3 upper sections and 2 lower ones)
OW
(L = three shapes inside one another; N = no shapes inside one another; O = two shapes inside one another; W = open moon facing left; P = black moon facing right; Q = black moon facing left)
The code should read:
LOOK BY POST BOX NOW

Pages 72–73
Challenge 1
Answers as follows from the top of page 72:
TR
(T = triangle in the top left corner is shaded towards the corner of the figure; Y = triangle in the top left corner is shaded towards the middle of the figure; B = bottom line is vertical; R = bottom line is diagonal)
YT
(Z = top right circle has a fine line; U = top right circle is dashed; Y = top right circle is bold; I = top right circle is dotted; E = all three semicircles have a bold line crossing them; T = left-hand semicircles have a bold line crossing them; F = right-hand semicircles have a bold line crossing them)
HE
(D = horizontal bold line on left side of figure; H = no bold line on left side of the figure; Q = sideways, bold v-shape on left side of the figure; E = heart in the orange shaded section; B = heart in blue shaded section; A = heart outside shaded sections)
WE
(V = starting with the top shape and moving clockwise, the shapes are square, circle, flower and triangle; W = starting with the top shape and moving clockwise, the shapes are triangle, flower, circle and square; E = top triangle shaded purple; F = bottom triangle shaded purple; G = both triangles shaded purple)
ST
(S = diamond shape; V = pentagon facing upwards; X = pentagon facing downwards; T = vertical shading; B = crosshatch shading; C = horizontal shading)
The code should read:
TRY THE WEST

Challenge 2

LK

(Q = number; L = letter; I = no symmetry;
J = vertical symmetry; K = horizontal
symmetry)
Based on initials, the culprit is Light-handed
Keith.

Pages 74–75
Challenge 1

a)–c) In each case, the flaps indicated
would appear to have disappeared. There
would be nothing showing outside the
main shape remaining as the flaps would all
have been tucked behind.

Challenge 2

a) D   b) A   c) A

Challenge 3

The answer should show the figures
appearing as the paper is unfolded. First
the figures will be mirrored as the paper
is folded down along its horizontal edge;
then the hexagon should be shown
appearing on the bottom left-hand corner;
then the hexagon should appear in the top
left-hand corner.

Challenge 4

a)   The unfolded paper should have a heart
     in the top right-hand corner (but not
     the bottom right-hand corner) and two
     circles central on the left-hand side.
b)   The unfolded paper should have two
     hearts arranged on the left-hand side
     arranged vertically (the upper one
     upside down), two hearts horizontally
     in the middle of the top side with the
     points facing outward, two squares
     either side of the central diagonal line
     and two hearts in the bottom right-
     hand corner arranged with their points
     inwards.

Now Try This!

1.   C
2.   a) E   b) A

Pages 76–77
Challenge 1

Answers will vary.

Challenge 2

a)   Clover and spiral; leaf and star; circle
     and heart.
b)   Dots and semiquaver; star and quaver;
     treble clef and bass clef.
c)   Sun and diamond; moon and circle;
     daisy and three dots.
d)   Diamond and moon; dots and circle;
     semiquaver and quaver.
e)   Bass clef and triangle; treble clef and
     daisy; spiral and diamond.
f)   Star and circles; moon and dots; circle
     and sun.
g)   Clover and daisy; spiral and diamond;
     circle and bass clef.
h)   Five-point star and sun; heart and leaf;
     circle and four-point star.
i)   Circle and heart; star and leaf; clover
     and moon.
j)   Daisy and treble clef; moon and dots;
     semiquaver and heart.
k)   Clover and four-point star; heart and
     sun; moon and dots.

Challenge 3

a)   B, D, E and H could be made from the
     net.

b)   i)–iii) Answers will vary.

Now Try This!

1.   a) B
     b) C
2.   a) D
     b) E

Pages 78–79
Challenge 1

a)   The rug's squares are A–P starting in
     the top left-hand corner and working
     from left to right across each row.
     Rotations: A, C, E, H, J, M, P
     Reflections: B, D, F, G, I, K, L, N, O.
b)   The rug's squares are A–P starting in
     the top left-hand corner and working
     from left to right across each row.
     Rotations: A, F, G, K, J, P
     Reflections: B, C, D, E, H, I, L, M, N, O.

Challenge 2

B

Challenge 3

a)–b) Both drawings should show the
originals reflected in a vertical mirror line.

Now Try This!

1.   C
2.   D
3.   C
4.   A
5.   A

Pages 80–81
Challenge 1

The hidden shapes are y, e, l, o and w.
The l appears twice to give hidden word
'yellow'.

Challenge 2

The shapes assemble as follows:
a)   Shape W at the top left: P at the
     bottom left; E on the right
b)   Shape R at the top left; O at the
     bottom left; F on the right
c)   Shape L at the top left; O at the
     bottom left; T at the bottom right; ! fits
     between L and T
The note should read 'yellow flower pot!'

Challenge 3

a) T   b) E   c) N

Now Try This!

1.   a) A, B, D
     b) A, B, C
2.   a) D
     b) A

Pages 82–83
Challenge 1

i = D   ii = A   iii = F

Challenge 2

i = B   ii = A   iii = D

Challenge 3

The blocks should show (all arranged
horizontally): two squares; five squares;
three squares; three squares

Now Try This!

1.   B
2.   E

Pages 84–88

1.   a) B
         Moving from left to right, the
         cross is added to the large shape
         and the lines change to dots.
         The large shape is reflected in a
         vertical mirror line.

     b) D
         Moving from left to right, the
         short diagonal line is reflected
         vertically; the central triangle
         changes to a pentagon; the
         elongated triangle changes to an
         elongated oval; the arrowheads
         become black-shaded.

2.   a) D
         Moving from left to right, the
         level of the horizontal line raises
         and lowers; the cross in the top
         left alternates between being
         present and vanishing; the circle
         moves left in each figure; the
         number of arrowheads increases
         by one in each figure.

     b) E
         Moving from left to right, the
         black shape vanishes each time.

3.   a) C
         A = arrowhead is large white;
         E = arrow going anticlockwise

     b) D
         Y = small triangle present rather
         than small square; W = shape at
         the top has more sides than the
         shape at the bottom

4.   a) E
         Moving from left to right, the
         polygons become regular and
         the shading swaps to the inside
         polygon. The line outside the large
         polygon at the top moves inside
         the large polygon to the bottom.
         The line outside the large polygon
         at the bottom moves inside the
         large polygon at the top.

     b) E
         Moving from left to right, the
         shading does not change. The
         image in the bottom right of the
         grid moves to the top left; the
         image in the top right of the grid
         rotates 90 degrees clockwise; the
         image in the bottom left of the
         grid moves to the bottom right
         and is reflected in a vertical mirror
         line; the image in the top left of
         the grid is reflected in a horizontal
         line and moves to the bottom left
         of the grid.

5.   a) D
         In each image on the left of the
         question, the small shapes follow
         the same order moving clockwise
         around the edge.

     b) E
         Both images on the left-hand side
         are identical but rotated.

6.   a) E
         In all the other figures, the arrow
         points to the cross.

     b) C
         In all the other figures, the circle is
         in a small triangle.

     c) E
         In all the other figures, there are
         six lines in total.

7.   a) A   b) C
8.   i) C   ii) A   iii) B
9.   a) D
     b) B

Test Paper 1
Pages 89–111
Section 1: Comprehension
1. **B**
   The questions do not require answers, so are rhetorical.
2. **C**
   This suggests that a lot of the narrator's description that follows is as if Anne is describing the scenery.
3. **D**
   The setting is so beautiful it is almost idealised or utopian.
4. **D**
   Anne has been in 'unlovely places' and is described by the narrator in sympathy as a 'poor child'.
5. **B**
   We are told she thinks about the brook in 'winter-time' and is highly observant.
6. **D**
   We are told about the beautiful fragrance from the trees.
7. **A**
   Marilla is practical as she tells Anne to hurry up and get dressed; she is not used to talking to children and therefore does not sound as kind as she means to.
8. **D**
   The fruits are 'small' and 'wormy'.
9. **C**
   'Upspringing' means the trees look as though they are springing up in 'scores'. A 'score' means about 20.
10. **B**
    The brook is described as 'laughing'.
11. **D**
    The field slopes down to the hollow.
12. **A**
    'Sparkling' is an adjective.
13. **A**
    She waves as if to include everything she can see.
14. **B**
    She savours the view so much she wants to see more of it.

Section 2: Shuffled Sentences
1. **E**   with
   Mum used a hammer to tap the nail in.
2. **C**   rehearsal
   Harriet always plays the piano beautifully.
3. **A**   on
   The farmer brings his cows in at milking time.
4. **B**   scissors
   The hairdresser has cut my hair too short.
5. **A**   after
   Finlay switches his laptop off every night before bed.
6. **D**   were
   Make sure you wear your waterproofs on the trip.
7. **C**   fell
   Heavy snow has fallen in the hills overnight.
8. **E**   some
   Faye dropped the hot pie on the kitchen floor.
9. **B**   in
   We walked round the edge of the lake before our picnic.
10. **A**   tend
    I always save the receipts of expensive purchases I make.
11. **C**   plate
    Raj likes to put tomato ketchup on his scrambled eggs.
12. **B**   flies
    A robin flew onto the bird table and pecked at the nuts.
13. **D**   past
    The villagers cheered as the royal carriages passed by.
14. **C**   such
    The food in the café was so salty we couldn't eat it.
15. **A**   taken
    I took lots of photos with my new camera when we were away.

Section 3: Numeracy
1. 22
   $3 \times 8 = 24$
   $24 - 2 = 22$
2. 21
   BODMAS so $6 \div 2 = 3$
   $24 - 3 = 21$
3. 25
   Add the two previous terms
   $9 + 16 = 25$
4. 11
   Even numbered positions are increasing by 3
   $8 + 3 = 11$
5. 96
   96 is divisible by 6 but not by 9
6. 12
   12 is not a factor of 64
7. 36
   $34 + 26 + 48 + 36 = 144$
   $144 \div 4 = 36$
8. 45
   39 to $-6 = 45$
9. 23
   The mode is the most common, so 23
10. 19
    The median is the middle number when put in order, so 19
11. 73
    $62 + 7 + 4 = 73$
12. 07
    $7:34 + 17 + 4 = 7:55$
    $7:55 + 1$ hour 12 minutes $= 9:07$
13. 14
    $11 + 3 = 14$

Section 4: Problem Solving
1. **D**   125
   $100 \div x = 80 \div 100$
   $10,000 \div x = 80$
   $x = 10,000 \div 80 = 125$
2. **B**   10
   $200 \div 4 = 50$
   $50 \times 0.2 = 10$
3. **D**   60
   Do the opposite in reverse, so
   $102 \times 2 = 204$
   $204 - 24 = 180$
   $180 \div 3 = 60$
4. **A**   76
   Ratio = 8 : 4 : 1
   Add the ratios to get 13

$247 \div 13 = 19$
$19 \times 4 = 76$
5. **E**   204 cm²
   Area of square = $14 \times 14 = 196$
   Area of rectangle = $40 \times 10 = 400$
   $400 - 196 = 204$
6. **C**   £74
   $14(3) + 8(4) = 74$
7. **E**   6 cm
   $6 \times 6 \times 6 = 216$
8. **A**   6,504.25
   $4.25 + 6,500 = 6,504.25$
9. **B**   £430
   $£850 \times 0.8 = 680$
   $680 - 250 = 430$
10. **D**   30p
    $3x + 4y = 2.70$
    $4x + 2y = 2.60$
    Double second equation to get
    $8x + 4y = 5.20$
    Subtract first equation to get
    $5x = 2.50$
    $x = 0.5$, substitute into first equation to get $1.50 + 4y = 2.70$, $4y = 1.20$, $y = 0.30$

Section 5: Synonyms
1. **E**   inquire
2. **D**   sparse
3. **A**   envy
4. **E**   affected
5. **C**   lean
6. **B**   extracted
7. **D**   wake
8. **A**   admit
9. **B**   abstain
10. **E**   harmless
11. **C**   unfriendly
12. **D**   luminous
13. **B**   clairvoyant
14. **D**   menacing
15. **A**   nationalistic
16. **C**   tire
17. **B**   poisonous
18. **E**   impartial
19. **B**   begin
20. **C**   touching
21. **A**   photographers
22. **E**   affectionate
23. **D**   department
24. **B**   container

Section 6: Non-Verbal Ability
1. **C**
2. **A**
3. **B**
4. **D**
5. **C**
6. **E**
7. **A**
8. **B**
   Moving from left to right, the large striped shape is duplicated and made smaller. The two shapes are aligned one above the other, with the upper shape's stripes rotated 90 degrees. The large white shape is also duplicated and made smaller. The small white shape is made tiny, shaded black and is put inside the duplicated white shapes.
9. **A**
   Moving from left to right, the shape is reflected in a mirror line that runs vertically alongside it and then rotated

90 degrees clockwise. The bottom shape is shaded black at either end and the top shape is shaded black in wedge shapes, narrower towards the middle line.

10. **A**

Moving from left to right, the component parts of the large shape are separated and arranged with three on the top row and two on the bottom row. On the top row, one shape is shaded grey and another black.

11. **E**

Moving from left to right, the shape is rotated 90 degrees anticlockwise. The heavy lines become fine; dashed lines become heavy; fine lines become dashed.

12. **E**

Moving from left to right, the figure is reflected in a vertical line.

13. **D**

Moving from left to right, white shading becomes black and all striped shading is rotated 90 degrees.

Test Paper 2
Pages 112–132
Section 1: Problem Solving
1. **I**   £13.50
   40.50 ÷ 3 = £13.50
2. **I**   £13.50
   £9.38 + (2.06 × 2) = £13.50
3. **F**   £14.50
   45 × 0.14 = £6.30
   £6.30 + £5.70 + £2.50 = £14.50
4. **A**   10:57 am
   8:22 + 94 minutes + 18 + 24 + 19
   = 10:57 am
5. **C**   2,500
   25 cm × 100 cm = 2,500 cm^2
6. **H**   500
   5 × 1 = 5
   2,500 ÷ 5 = 500
7. **D**   50
   12p for first 5 minutes
   £1.47 − 12p = £1.35
   1.35 ÷ 0.03 = 45 minutes
   45 + 5 = 50 minutes
8. **E**   250
   50 × 5 = 250 cm^2
9. **J**   45
   2 hours and 16 minutes
   = 136 minutes
   136 ÷ 4 = 34 minutes
   34 + 11 = 45 minutes
10. **A**   10:57 am
   12:14 − 1 hour and 17 minutes
   = 10:57 am

Section 2: Cloze
1. **H**   monarchs
2. **J**   fun
3. **B**   contrast
4. **G**   boring
5. **D**   lavish
6. **E**   indulgence
7. **A**   toll
8. **F**   eventually
9. **I**   perhaps
10. **C**   wives
11. **D**   border
12. **J**   peak

13. **G**   summit
14. **A**   challenge
15. **B**   expedition
16. **C**   known
17. **E**   referred
18. **I**   rapidity
19. **F**   perilous
20. **H**   extreme

Section 3: Non-Verbal Ability
1. **D**   MRS
   L = brickwork pattern has two bricks on top and bottom row, three in the middle; M = brickwork pattern has three bricks on top and bottom row, two in the middle; N = brickwork pattern has two bricks on the bottom rows, three on the top; P = black dot in top right-hand corner; Q = black dot in top left-hand corner; R = dot in middle of top row; S = dot is not below black triangle; T = dot is directly below black triangle
2. **C**   TU
   T = white rectangle layered in the middle of all the shapes; Y = white rectangle layered at the front of all the shapes; U = dotted square; Q = white square; O = diagonally striped square
3. **E**   IRM
   I = odd number of crosses; G = even number of crosses; K = black dot inside star is on right-hand side of figure; R = black dot inside star is on left-hand side of figure; M = black dot outside star at top right-hand side; N = black dot outside star at bottom right-hand side; O = black dot outside star at bottom
4. **A**   FKW
   F = zig-zag scallops; U = curved scallops; J = 6 scallops; Q = 8 scallops; K = 7 scallops; W = dot in right-hand circle; Z = vertical line in right-hand circle; X = horizontal line in right-hand circle
5. **E**   OTN
   O = diagonal shading going from top left to bottom right; P = diagonal shading going from bottom left to top right; R = small rectangle aligned to the left in the square; S = small rectangle aligned to the middle in the square; T = small rectangle aligned to the right in the square; M = irregular hexagon in the square; N = irregular pentagon in the square
6. **B**   DWB
   D = no loops in the outer shape; P = one loop in the outer shape; V = two loops in the outer shape; Z = three circles in total; W = four circles in total; A = two black circles; B = three black circles
7. **A**   FAN
   F = two scallops; X = three scallops; E = four scallops; U = three black circles inside the shape; O = two black circles and one white circle inside the shape; A = two black circles and two white circles inside the shape; N = arrow points to the black circle outside the shape; M = arrow points to the scallops outside the shape; P = arrow does not

point to scallop or black circle outside the shape
8. **A**   ENQ
   B = diagonal striped shading running from bottom left to top right in the outer shape; E = vertical striped shading in the outer shape; Y = diagonal striped shading running from bottom right to top left in the outer shape; S = arrow pointing towards the centre shape; M = arrow pointing away from the centre shape; N = double-headed arrow; O = no arrowheads; Q = black dot in the centre of a side; R = black dot touching a corner of the figure
9. **E**
10. **G**
11. **A**
12. **D**
13. **C**
14. **F**
15. **B**

Section 4: Grammar and Spelling
1. **A**   break
2. **D**   im
3. **B**   marraige
   The correct spelling is 'marriage'.
4. **C**   adjective
5. **E**   fast
6. **B**   aquisition
   The correct spelling is 'acquisition'.
7. ac**ou**stic
8. courag**eou**s
9. defin**ite**ly
10. con**sci**ousness

Section 5: Antonyms
1. **C**   stingy
2. **D**   base
3. **A**   impotent
4. **E**   repel
5. **B**   precede
6. **D**   relapse
7. **B**   lenient
8. **E**   contempt
9. **A**   hide
10. **E**   elevate
11. **C**   ornate
12. **D**   feeble
13. **B**   tough
14. **D**   important
15. **C**   certainty

Section 6: Numeracy
1. **C**   16y + 12
   4(4y + 3) = 16y + 12
2. **E**   225 cm^2
   4(3) + 3 = 15
   15 × 15 = 225
3. **E**   12.5 cm
   25 ÷ 2 = 12.5
4. **A** $\frac{19}{20}$
   $\frac{16}{20} + \frac{3}{20} = \frac{19}{20}$
5. **A** $\frac{1}{2}$
   $\frac{2}{3} \times \frac{3}{4} = \frac{6}{12} = \frac{1}{2}$
6. **D** $\frac{13}{30}$
   $\frac{18}{30} - \frac{5}{30} = \frac{13}{30}$

7. C $\frac{1}{36}$

$\frac{1}{6} \times \frac{1}{6} = \frac{1}{36}$

8. C 75°

$360 \div 60 = 6$

$12.5 \times 6 = 75$

9. C 2

A rhombus and a square

10. C 30

$9,000 \div 300 = 30$

11. A 6:54 am

2 hours 15 minutes + 36 minutes
= 2 hours 51 minutes
9:45 am – 2 hours 51 minutes
= 6:54 am

12. B 10%

$13 + 3 + 12 + 4 + 2 + 4 + 6 + 16 = 60$
$6 \div 60 = 10\%$

13. D $\frac{13}{30}$

$16 + 4 + 2 + 4 = 26$
$26 \div 60 = 13 \div 30$

14. B 243

$6 \times 6 \times 6 = 216$
$3 \times 3 \times 3 = 27$
$216 + 27 = 243$

15. A 106

Add the previous two terms, so
$41 + 65 = 106$

16. E 180 cm²

$(4 \times 3) \div 2 = 6$
$3 \times 14 = 42$
$14 \times 5 = 70$
$14 \times 4 = 56$
$6 + 6 + 42 + 70 + 56 = 180$

17. A 17

Do the opposite in reverse, so
$97 - 29 = 68$
$68 \div 4 = 17$

18. D £11.60

12 noon – 8 pm = 8 hours,
$8 \div 2 = 4$, $4 \times 2.50 = 10$
8 pm – 10 pm = 2 hours,
$2 \times 80p = £1.60$
£10 + £1.60 = £11.60

Test Paper 3
Pages 133–155
Section 1: Comprehension

1. B

The men will 'put up' near Shiplake islands.

2. A

Initially, the narrator and Harris peel the potato until it is only the size of a 'peanut'.

3. D

The narrator and Harris are both entirely covered in potato peelings so evidently have not been economic or careful.

4. B

The men cannot believe how much mess was made from just four potatoes.

5. D

There is the first peeled potato that is reduced in size dramatically, four scraped potatoes and 'half-a-dozen or so' unpeeled potatoes.

6. D

The stew includes 'the odds and ends and the remnants' and the narrator tells us 'I forget the other ingredients'.

7. A

The men are eager cooks but not tidy or efficient.

8. C

George directs the narrator and Harris in what they are doing.

9. B

The writer creates a humorous tone in showing how the narrator and his friends are not competent campers.

10. A

The narrator jokes that Montmorency is contributing a rat for the pot.

11. C

The suggestion is that George's reluctance to try something new is indicative of a type of cautious person who does not help the development of new ideas.

12. B

A 'slap-up' meal is a bit more special than usual.

13. D

A remnant is a left-over scrap.

14. B

Montmorency demonstrated 'great interest in the proceedings'.

Section 2: Odd One Out

1. C fragrant
The others relate to unpleasant smells.

2. D harmony
The others relate to something disagreeable.

3. E sombre
The others relate to light.

4. A pallid
The others relate to a strong or deep colour.

5. D expectantly
The others relate to something that happens suddenly.

6. C Italy
The others are languages.

7. B soul
The others are parts of a shoe or boot.

8. C ethereal
The others describe a solid, tangible material, whereas ethereal is something delicate and not of this world.

9. B prefix
A prefix is added to a word to change its meaning; the others refer to words in their own right.

10. E reciprocate
The others relate to jerky movements.

11. D denial
The others relate to belief.

12. A inane
The others relate to being clever.

13. C repose
The others relate to expending effort.

14. B speech
The others relate to advice.

15. D artless
The others relate to craftiness.

Section 3: Numeracy

1. 52
$14 + 23 + 15 = 52$

2. 27
$75 \div 5 = 15$
$15 + 12 = 27$

3. 63
Add 1 less each time, so $56 + 7 = 63$

4. 69
$108 - 39 = 69$

5. 02
12 and 24 so 2

6. 55
$1 + 4 + 9 + 16 + 25 = 55$

7. 77
$6 \times 48 = 288$
$24 + 99 + 88 = 211$
$288 - 211 = 77$

8. 00
Mode is most so 0

9. 99
$99 - 0 = 99$

10. 22
Ratio = 6 : 2 : 1
Add ratios to get 9
$99 \div 9 = 11$
$11 \times 2 = 22$

11. 12
$\frac{1}{14}$ of 7 days = 0.5 days
$0.5 \times 24 = 12$

12. 44
$5 \times 5 \times 5 = 125$
$9 \times 9 = 81$
$125 - 81 = 44$

13. 80
$60 + 20 = 80$

14. 03
$1 + 1 + 0 + 0 + 0 + 1 = 3$

15. 35
Add the previous two, so $22 + 13 = 35$

16. 13
$-5 + 24 - 6 = 13$

17. 35
8:49 am to 9:24 am = 35 minutes

18. 60
LCM of 12 and 15 = 60

Section 4: Non-Verbal Ability

1. C

2. E

3. D

4. A

5. A

6. E

7. D

8. C
The figures on the left-hand side both have an arrow positioned at the bottom right-hand side of a small rectangle, with a diagonal line also appearing adjacent to the figure. There are diagonal lines cutting through the rectangle in the figure.

9. E
The figures on the left-hand side both have a larger shape and a medium sized shape; the medium shape has three fewer sides than the large shape.

10. A
The figures on the left-hand side both have a small circle and a small cross directly opposite one another.

11. A
The figures on the left-hand side both have an open circle in the bottom right-hand brick, a patterned shading in the bottom left-hand brick and a small black shape at the edge of one brick. There is a triangle at the top of the figure, the shading of which matches the long thin horizontal rectangle at the bottom of the figure.

12. A
The two figures on the left-hand side are both made up of a quarter circle with a solid parallel line in alignment with one of the straight sides. There is an arrow pointing to the top left of the figure as it cuts through the main shape and a dashed line at the base of the figure.

13. D
The two figures on the left-hand side of the question have a triangle with diagonal striped shading from the bottom left to top right.

14. D
The figures on the left-hand side both have a number of short perpendicular lines cutting through the outer shape equal to the number of circles inside the shape.

Section 5: Word Definitions

1. B   mournfully
'Dolefully' means sadly.

2. E   notorious
'Infamous' means to be well known for a bad quality.

3. E   beautiful
'Exquisite' means extraordinarily charming.

4. A   lumberjack
An 'arborist' is a tree surgeon, one of whose jobs is to fell trees. 'Lumberjack' is the closest meaning.

5. D   waving
'Brandishing' means holding aloft/ waving in the air.

6. E   genuine
'Authentic' means real.

7. B   unclear
'Oblique' means not explicit/in a roundabout way.

8. B   obvious
'Blatant' means unconcealed.

9. A   irrevocable
'Irreparable' means impossible to fix.

10. E   surpassed
'Exceeded' means went beyond.

11. E   concurrence
'Consensus' means agreement.

12. D   chastised
'Reproached' means scolded.

13. C   compulsory
'Obligatory' means required.

14. B   careless
'Negligent' means neglectful.

15. A   motionless
'Inert' means not moving.

Section 6: Problem Solving

1. B   one-eighth
$1 - \dfrac{3}{4} = \dfrac{1}{4}$

$\dfrac{1}{2} \times \dfrac{1}{4} = \dfrac{1}{8}$

2. D   20%
$\dfrac{1}{5} = \dfrac{20}{100}$

3. A   126°
$x = 48 + 39 = 87$
$y = 180 - 48 - (180 - 87) = 39$
$87 + 39 = 126$

4. E   32x + 16
$8x + 3 + 8x + 3 + 8x + 5 + 8x + 5$
$= 32x + 16$

5. D   £2.45
$840 \div 24 = 35p$
$35p \times 7 = £2.45$

6. E   £4.97
$3 \times £3.75 = £11.25$
$£2.18 + £1.60 = £3.78$
$£20 - £11.25 - £3.78 = £4.97$

7. C   59
BODMAS so $30 \div 2 = 15$, $44 + 15 = 59$

8. D   135°
$360 \div 60 = 6$
$6 \times 22.5 = 135$

9. A   10.39
$8.92 + 1.47 = 10.39$

10. E   (3, −2)

11. B   82
$82 - 58 = 24$
$58 + 24 = 82$

12. C   75 miles
8:20 am to 9:50 am = 1.5 hours
$50 \times 1.5 = 75$

13. D   £1
$3x + 4y = 7.60$
$2x + 8y = 10.40$
Double first equation to get
$6x + 8y = 15.20$
Subtract second equation to get
$4x = 4.80$, $x = 1.20$
Put into first equation to get
$3(1.20) + 4y = 7.60$
$3.60 + 4y = 7.60$
$4y = 4$, $y = 1$

THIS PAGE HAS DELIBERATELY BEEN LEFT BLANK

THIS PAGE HAS DELIBERATELY BEEN LEFT BLANK

Pupil's Full Name:

Instructions:
Mark the boxes correctly like this ▲

Please sign your name here:

Section 1: Comprehension

Example i

   Ⓐ   Ⓑ   Ⓒ   ◉

Example ii

   Ⓐ   Ⓑ   Ⓒ   Ⓓ

1 Ⓐ Ⓑ Ⓒ Ⓓ
2 Ⓐ Ⓑ Ⓒ Ⓓ
3 Ⓐ Ⓑ Ⓒ Ⓓ
4 Ⓐ Ⓑ Ⓒ Ⓓ
5 Ⓐ Ⓑ Ⓒ Ⓓ
6 Ⓐ Ⓑ Ⓒ Ⓓ
7 Ⓐ Ⓑ Ⓒ Ⓓ
8 Ⓐ Ⓑ Ⓒ Ⓓ
9 Ⓐ Ⓑ Ⓒ Ⓓ
10 Ⓐ Ⓑ Ⓒ Ⓓ
11 Ⓐ Ⓑ Ⓒ Ⓓ
12 Ⓐ Ⓑ Ⓒ Ⓓ
13 Ⓐ Ⓑ Ⓒ Ⓓ
14 Ⓐ Ⓑ Ⓒ Ⓓ

Section 2: Shuffled Sentences

Example i

  Ⓐ ◉ Ⓒ Ⓓ Ⓔ

Example ii

  Ⓐ Ⓑ Ⓒ Ⓓ Ⓔ

1 Ⓐ Ⓑ Ⓒ Ⓓ Ⓔ
2 Ⓐ Ⓑ Ⓒ Ⓓ Ⓔ
3 Ⓐ Ⓑ Ⓒ Ⓓ Ⓔ
4 Ⓐ Ⓑ Ⓒ Ⓓ Ⓔ
5 Ⓐ Ⓑ Ⓒ Ⓓ Ⓔ
6 Ⓐ Ⓑ Ⓒ Ⓓ Ⓔ
7 Ⓐ Ⓑ Ⓒ Ⓓ Ⓔ
8 Ⓐ Ⓑ Ⓒ Ⓓ Ⓔ
9 Ⓐ Ⓑ Ⓒ Ⓓ Ⓔ
10 Ⓐ Ⓑ Ⓒ Ⓓ Ⓔ
11 Ⓐ Ⓑ Ⓒ Ⓓ Ⓔ
12 Ⓐ Ⓑ Ⓒ Ⓓ Ⓔ
13 Ⓐ Ⓑ Ⓒ Ⓓ Ⓔ
14 Ⓐ Ⓑ Ⓒ Ⓓ Ⓔ
15 Ⓐ Ⓑ Ⓒ Ⓓ Ⓔ

Section 3: Numeracy

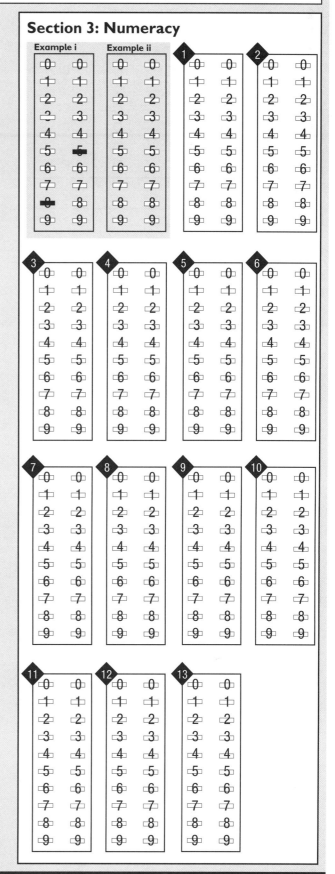

Section 4: Problem Solving

Example i

	A	B	C	D	E

Example ii

	A	B	C	D	E

	A	B	C	D	E
1	A	B	C	D	E
2	A	B	C	D	E
3	A	B	C	D	E
4	A	B	C	D	E
5	A	B	C	D	E
6	A	B	C	D	E
7	A	B	C	D	E
8	A	B	C	D	E
9	A	B	C	D	E
10	A	B	C	D	E

Section 5: Synonyms

Example i

	A	B	C	D	E

Example ii

	A	B	C	D	E

	A	B	C	D	E
1	A	B	C	D	E
2	A	B	C	D	E
3	A	B	C	D	E
4	A	B	C	D	E
5	A	B	C	D	E
6	A	B	C	D	E
7	A	B	C	D	E
8	A	B	C	D	E
9	A	B	C	D	E
10	A	B	C	D	E
11	A	B	C	D	E
12	A	B	C	D	E
13	A	B	C	D	E
14	A	B	C	D	E
15	A	B	C	D	E
16	A	B	C	D	E
17	A	B	C	D	E
18	A	B	C	D	E
19	A	B	C	D	E
20	A	B	C	D	E
21	A	B	C	D	E
22	A	B	C	D	E
23	A	B	C	D	E
24	A	B	C	D	E

Section 6: Non-Verbal Ability

Example i

	A	B	C	D	E

Example ii

	A	B	C	D	E

	A	B	C	D	E
1	A	B	C	D	E
2	A	B	C	D	E
3	A	B	C	D	E
4	A	B	C	D	E
5	A	B	C	D	E
6	A	B	C	D	E
7	A	B	C	D	E
8	A	B	C	D	E
9	A	B	C	D	E
10	A	B	C	D	E
11	A	B	C	D	E
12	A	B	C	D	E
13	A	B	C	D	E

Pupil's Full Name:

Instructions:
Mark the boxes correctly like this ▲

Please sign your name here:

Section 1: Problem Solving

Example i

A B C D E F G H I J

Example ii

A B C D E F G H I J

1   A B C D E F G H I J
2   A B C D E F G H I J
3   A B C D E F G H I J
4   A B C D E F G H I J
5   A B C D E F G H I J
6   A B C D E F G H I J
7   A B C D E F G H I J
8   A B C D E F G H I J
9   A B C D E F G H I J
10 A B C D E F G H I J

Section 2: Cloze

Example i

A B C D E

Example ii

A B C D E

1   A B C D E F G H I J
2   A B C D E F G H I J
3   A B C D E F G H I J
4   A B C D E F G H I J
5   A B C D E F G H I J
6   A B C D E F G H I J
7   A B C D E F G H I J
8   A B C D E F G H I J
9   A B C D E F G H I J
10 A B C D E F G H I J
11 A B C D E F G H I J
12 A B C D E F G H I J
13 A B C D E F G H I J
14 A B C D E F G H I J
15 A B C D E F G H I J
16 A B C D E F G H I J
17 A B C D E F G H I J
18 A B C D E F G H I J
19 A B C D E F G H I J
20 A B C D E F G H I J

Section 3: Non-Verbal Ability

Example i

A B C D E

Example ii

A B

Example iii

A B

1   A B C D E
2   A B C D E
3   A B C D E
4   A B C D E
5   A B C D E
6   A B C D E
7   A B C D E
8   A B C D E

9   A B C D E F G
10 A B C D E F G
11 A B C D E F G
12 A B C D E F G
13 A B C D E F G
14 A B C D E F G
15 A B C D E F G

Section 4: Grammar and Spelling

Example i

A B C D E

Example ii

A B C D E

1 A B C D E
2 A B C D E
3 A B C D E
4 A B C D E
5 A B C D E
6 A B C D E
7
8
9
10

Section 5: Antonyms

Example i

A B C D E

Example ii

A B C D E

1 A B C D E
2 A B C D E
3 A B C D E
4 A B C D E
5 A B C D E
6 A B C D E
7 A B C D E
8 A B C D E
9 A B C D E
10 A B C D E
11 A B C D E
12 A B C D E
13 A B C D E
14 A B C D E
15 A B C D E

Section 6: Numeracy

Example i

A B C D E

Example ii

A B C D E

1 A B C D E
2 A B C D E
3 A B C D E
4 A B C D E
5 A B C D E
6 A B C D E
7 A B C D E
8 A B C D E
9 A B C D E
10 A B C D E
11 A B C D E
12 A B C D E
13 A B C D E
14 A B C D E
15 A B C D E
16 A B C D E
17 A B C D E
18 A B C D E

Pupil's Full Name:

Instructions:
Mark the boxes correctly like this 🖪

Please sign your name here:

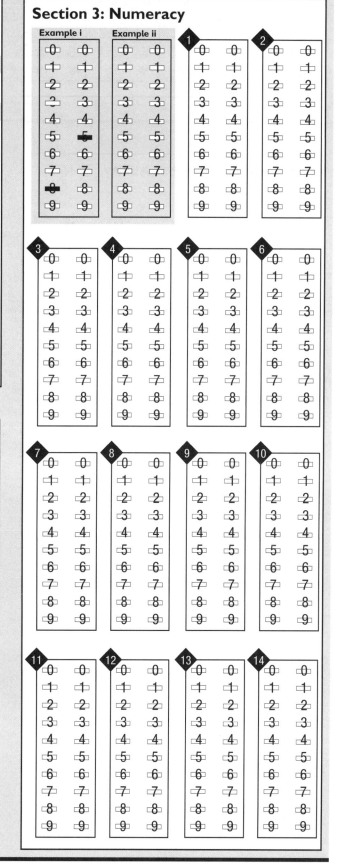

Section 1: Comprehension

Example i

	A	B	C	D

Example ii

	A	B	C	D
1	A	B	C	D
2	A	B	C	D
3	A	B	C	D
4	A	B	C	D
5	A	B	C	D
6	A	B	C	D
7	A	B	C	D
8	A	B	C	D
9	A	B	C	D
10	A	B	C	D
11	A	B	C	D
12	A	B	C	D
13	A	B	C	D
14	A	B	C	D

Section 2: Odd One Out

Example i

	A	B	C	D	E

Example ii

	A	B	C	D	E
1	A	B	C	D	E
2	A	B	C	D	E
3	A	B	C	D	E
4	A	B	C	D	E
5	A	B	C	D	E
6	A	B	C	D	E
7	A	B	C	D	E
8	A	B	C	D	E
9	A	B	C	D	E
10	A	B	C	D	E
11	A	B	C	D	E
12	A	B	C	D	E
13	A	B	C	D	E
14	A	B	C	D	E
15	A	B	C	D	E

Section 3: Numeracy

Section 3: Numeracy (continued)

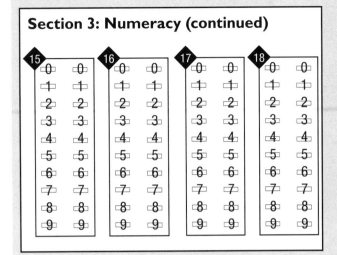

Section 4: Non-Verbal Ability

Example i

	A	B	C	D	E

Example ii

	A	B	C	D	E
1	A	B	C	D	E
2	A	B	C	D	E
3	A	B	C	D	E
4	A	B	C	D	E
5	A	B	C	D	E
6	A	B	C	D	E
7	A	B	C	D	E
8	A	B	C	D	E
9	A	B	C	D	E
10	A	B	C	D	E
11	A	B	C	D	E
12	A	B	C	D	E
13	A	B	C	D	E
14	A	B	C	D	E

Section 5: Word Definitions

Example i

	A	B	C	D	E

Example ii

	A	B	C	D	E
1	A	B	C	D	E
2	A	B	C	D	E
3	A	B	C	D	E
4	A	B	C	D	E
5	A	B	C	D	E
6	A	B	C	D	E
7	A	B	C	D	E
8	A	B	C	D	E
9	A	B	C	D	E
10	A	B	C	D	E
11	A	B	C	D	E
12	A	B	C	D	E
13	A	B	C	D	E
14	A	B	C	D	E
15	A	B	C	D	E

Section 6: Problem Solving

Example i

	A	B	C	D	E

Example ii

	A	B	C	D	E
1	A	B	C	D	E
2	A	B	C	D	E
3	A	B	C	D	E
4	A	B	C	D	E
5	A	B	C	D	E
6	A	B	C	D	E
7	A	B	C	D	E
8	A	B	C	D	E
9	A	B	C	D	E
10	A	B	C	D	E
11	A	B	C	D	E
12	A	B	C	D	E
13	A	B	C	D	E